Feminist Practice
and
Poststructuralist Theory

Feminist Practice
and
Poststructuralist Theory

CHRIS WEEDON

Basil Blackwell

Copyright © Chris Weedon 1987

First published 1987
Reprinted 1988, 1989

Basil Blackwell Ltd
108 Cowley Road, Oxford OX4 1JF, UK

Basil Blackwell Inc.
432 Park Avenue South, Suite 1503
New York, NY 10016, USA

British Library Cataloguing in Publication Data

Weedon, Chris
    Feminist practice and poststructuralist
    theory.
    1. Structuralism
    I. Title
    149'.96   B841.4
    ISBN 0-631-15069-2
    ISBN 0-631-15188-5 Pbk

Library of Congress Cataloging in Publication Data

Weedon, Chris.
    Feminist practice and poststructuralist theory.
    Bibliography: p.
    Includes index.
    1. Femininsm.   2. Structuralism.   I. Title.
    II. Title: Feminist practice and post-structuralist
    theory.
    HQ1154.W42   1987   305.4'2   87–11567
    ISBN 0-631-15069-2
    ISBN 0-631-15188-5 (pbk.)

Typeset in 10½ on 12pt Garamond
by Cambrian Typesetters, Frimley, Surrey
Printed in Great Britain by
Billing and Sons Ltd., Worcester

Contents

Acknowledgements

The author and publishers are grateful to the following for permission to reproduce extracts: to The Harvester Press/Wheatsheaf Books Ltd and The University of Massachusetts Press for lines from *New French Feminisms* (Brighton: Harvester, 1981) edited by Elaine Marks and Isabelle de Courtivron, copyright © 1980 by The University of Massachusetts Press; and to Pantheon Books (a division of Random House Inc.) and Penguin Books for lines from *The History of Sexuality, Volume One, An Introduction* (Harmondsworth: Pelican, 1981) by Michel Foucault, translated by Robert Hurley (Allen Lane, 1979), copyright © Editions Gallimard, 1976, translation copyright © 1978 by Random House Inc., reproduced by permission of Pantheon Books and Penguin Books Ltd.

Preface

The aim of this book is to make poststructuralist theory accessible to readers to whom it is unfamiliar, to argue its political usefulness to feminism and to consider its implications for feminist critical practice. By feminist critical practice I mean ways of understanding social and cultural practices which throw light on how gender power relations are constituted, reproduced and contested. I begin by considering the relationship between feminism as a politics, both of the personal and the social, and theory. Chapter 1 suggests that the feminist focus on women's experience which brings together the personal and the political is extremely important but requires further theorization. Poststructuralist theories of language, subjectivity, discourse and power seem to me to offer useful ways of understanding experience and relating it to social power. Chapter 2 outlines the key principles of poststructuralist theory and these are taken up and developed further in chapters 3, 4 and 5. Chapter 3 focuses on psychoanalysis, chapter 4 on language and subjectivity and chapter 5 on discourse and power. In the final chapter a poststructuralist framework is applied to the institution and practices of literary criticism in an attempt to demonstrate the explanatory power and political usefulness of this theory and to point to a possible direction for future feminist cultural criticism.

I wish to thank all those who have assisted me in the writing of this book, particularly Catherine Belsey who has been extremely helpful and supportive throughout. Special thanks are also due to Gill Boden, Jane Moore and Teresa Rees who provided useful comments on the manuscript and to Philip Carpenter of Blackwell for his support.

1

Feminism and Theory

Feminism and Politics

Feminism is a politics. It is a politics directed at changing existing power relations between women and men in society. These power relations structure all areas of life, the family, education and welfare, the worlds of work and politics, culture and leisure. They determine who does what and for whom, what we are and what we might become.

Like all politics contemporary feminism has its roots in a political movement, the Women's Liberation Movement, which has been an active force for change since the late 1960s. The concerns of the Women's Liberation Movement are many and affect every aspect of women's lives. They include the very question of what it is to be a woman, how our femininity and our sexuality are defined for us and how we might begin to redefine them for ourselves. They include campaigns against the objectification of women as sexual objects for male consumption, against pornography, rape and other forms of violence against women within and outside the family. The Women's Liberation Movement is concerned with education, welfare rights, equality of opportunity, pay and conditions, the social provision of childcare and the right to choose freely whether and when to have children. It is concerned with the way in which the oppressions of patriarchy are compounded for many women by class and race.[1] These political questions should be the motivating force behind feminist theory which must always be answerable to the needs of women in our struggle to transform patriarchy.

As feminists we take as our starting point the *patriarchal* structure of society. The term 'patriarchal' refers to power relations in which women's interests are subordinated to the interests of men. These power relations take many forms, from the sexual division of labour and the social organization of procreation to the internalized norms of femininity by which we live. Patriarchal power rests on the social meanings given to biological sexual difference. In patriarchal discourse the nature and social role of women are defined in relation to a norm which is male. This finds its clearest expression in the generic use of the terms 'man' and 'he' to encompass all of humankind. Many of the social and political gains made by women over the last 100 years have been the result of struggles to include women in the rights and privileges which men have instituted to serve their own interests. Yet women's inclusion in education, the franchise, public life and the labour market have been on terms designed to meet the needs of individual men, unfettered by ties of motherhood, childcare and domestic labour. Women seeking inclusion have had to negotiate the conflicting demands made upon them by their dual role as best they could on an individual basis.

Behind the general unwillingness, except among feminists, to rethink the sexual division of labour and its implications for the equality of women and men lies a fundamental patriarchal assumption that women's biological difference from men fits them for different social tasks. In liberal democracies, this assumption finds its expression in discriminatory social policies. It is difficult, for example, for men to play a full role in childcare when they are not entitled to parental leave or for women to succeed in career structures which do not take account of parental responsibility. Much of British educational and welfare provision is implicitly organized on the assumption that women are 'equal but different'. It is not that we are not as important and valuable as men, but that we are *naturally* equipped to fulfil different social functions, primarily those of wife and mother. Being a good wife and mother, as these roles are currently defined, calls for particular qualities, thought to be naturally feminine, such as patience, emotion and self-sacrifice. These expectations about natural femininity structure women's access to the labour market and to public life. Common sense tells us that women are best suited to the service industries and 'caring' professions and that the 'aggressive' worlds of management, decision-making and politics call for masculine qualities even in a woman. Yet are masculine qualities in a woman quite natural?

To say that patriarchal relations are *structural* is to suggest that they exist in the institutions and social practices of our society and cannot be explained by the intentions, good or bad, of individual women or men. This is not to deny that individual women and men are often the agents of oppression but to suggest that we need a theory which can explain how and why people oppress each other, a theory of subjectivity, of conscious and unconscious thoughts and emotions, which can account for the relationship between the individual and the social. The social institutions which we enter as individuals – for example, the family, schools and colleges, teenage fashion and pop culture, the church and the worlds of work and leisure – pre-exist us. We learn their modes of operation and the values which they seek to maintain as true, natural or good. As children we learn what girls and boys should be and, later, women and men. These subject positions – ways of being an individual – and the values inherent in them may not all be compatible and we will learn that we can choose between them. As women we have a range of possibilities. In theory almost every walk of life is open to us, but all the possibilities which we share with men involve accepting, negotiating or rejecting what is constantly being offered to us as our primary role – that of wife and mother. Whatever else we do, we should be attractive and desirable to men, and, ideally, our sexuality should be given to one man and our emotional energy directed at him and the children of the marriage. This message comes to us from a wide range of sources, for instance, children's books, women's magazines, religion, the advertising industry, romance, television, the cinema and current tax and social security arrangements.

Many women and more men would say: 'but that's only

natural'. To describe contemporary social relations as natural is, of course, one way of understanding them. The appeal to the 'natural' is one of the most powerful aspects of *common-sense* thinking, but it is a way of understanding social relations which denies history and the possibility of change for the future. While no feminist would subscribe to such a position, there is a range of ways of understanding the meanings and implications of patriarchy from within feminism. These different ways of perceiving patriarchy result in different forms of feminist politics – liberal, separatist and socialist. Liberal feminism aims to achieve full equality of opportunity in all spheres of life without radically transforming the present social and political system. The realization of its aims, however, will mean the transformation of the sexual division of labour and of contemporary norms of femininity and masculinity. It will also require provision for domestic labour and childcare outside the nuclear family. Radical feminism envisages a new social order in which women will not be subordinated to men and femininity and femaleness will not be debased and devalued. In the short term, for radical feminists the only way in which women can assert their autonomy from men and recover their true and natural femininity is in separation from men and the patriarchal structures of society. For socialist feminists, patriarchy, as a social system, is integrally tied in with class and racial oppressions and can only be abolished through a full transformation of the social system. Socialist feminism does not envisage a true and natural femaleness, but sees gender as socially produced and historically changing.[2]

Politics and Theory

If feminism is a politics, it is also a theory, or rather a range of theories. Whether acknowledged or not, every form of feminist politics, and there are many, implies a particular way of understanding patriarchy and the possibilities of change. Theory, in this sense, is often implicit. Feminist perspectives on patriarchy will involve assumptions about sex, gender, femininity, masculinity, lesbianism, identity and change. The ways in which we understand these things will be derived from a range of sources and forms of knowledge production which may well be far from coherent. For many women, a feminist perspective results from the conflict and contradictions between dominant institutionalized definitions of women's nature and social role, inherent in the contemporary sexual division of labour, the structure of the family, access to work and politics, medicine, social welfare, religion and the media (to name but a few of the institutions defining femininity and womanhood) and our experience of these institutions in the context of the dominant liberal discourse of the free and self-determining individual. In order to make sense of these contradictions we need new theoretical perspectives which challenge individualism. It is here that feminist theories can make sense of women's awareness of the conflicts and contradictions in our everyday lives which, from the perspective of an isolated individual, who does not consciously take the social construction of gender into account, may seem inexplicable. Viewed from the perspective of women as a social group, they can produce new ways of seeing which make sense of them, enabling women to call them into question and open the way for change.

Yet recognizing contradictions and the power relations and interests which inhere in specific definitions of women's nature and social role is only the first stage in the process of change both for individual women and in the struggle to transform social institutions. This process requires the development of alternative senses of ourselves as women, and strategies for transforming existing institutions and practices. The range of contemporary feminisms offers different ways of seeing ourselves as women and implies different long-term strategies for change. In the short term, however, the immediate constraints of women's situations have created a large degree of co-operation between feminists of all kinds on strategies for tackling pressing issues such as the sexual division of labour, control of sexuality and violence against women.

Most feminists assume an integral relationship between theory and practice. Starting from the politics of the personal, in which women's subjectivities and experiences of everyday life become the site of the redefinition of patriarchal meanings and values and of resistance to them, feminism generates new theoretical perspectives from which the dominant can be criticized and new possibilities envisaged. Recent feminist theory, like its historical precursors, has developed through a critique of the patriarchal values and interests informing existing social theories. Feminism questions the assumptions about women which social theories posit as true, pointing to their irrelevance to women's experience or highlighting the frequent absence of women from them. The last fifteen years have seen various attempts to systematize individual insights about the oppression of women into relatively coherent theories of patriarchy based on specific definitions of femaleness and femininity. These have included radical-feminist, socialist-feminist and psychoanalytic-feminist theories. Other attempts have been made to add the 'problem' of women and the sexual division of labour to pre-existing bodies of theory, as in the case of liberalism and Marxism. In each instance, the overall theorization has implications for feminist practice which we cannot afford to ignore. One of the strengths of poststructuralist approaches is that they enable us to attend to the practical implications of particular ways of theorizing women's oppression and to recognize that feminist politics are crucial in determining which existing theories might be useful in the fight for change.

Theory and Experience

Yet many feminists maintain an active hostility to theory. It is seen as a way of denying the centrality of women's experience, a way of removing the control of the meaning of our lives from individual women and of telling us what we should think. It is seen as reinforcing the inequalities between women to which differential access to knowledge gives rise. Others, particularly influential radical-feminist writers like Mary Daly and Susan Griffin, see it as a masculine form of discourse which maintains male dominance by co-opting women and suppressing the feminine. These arguments link dominant western forms of rationality with male power and control over women and nature, a power which is associated with violence, oppression and destruction. Male violence is seen as relying on the suppression of the feminine which may take many forms, for example, the suppression of lesbianism, the male definition of female sexuality and, as Mary Daly argues in *Gyn/Ecology* (1979), the persecution of women as witches, practices such as Chinese footbinding, cliterodectomy, Indian *suttee* and contemporary gynaecology. The feminist critique of patriarchal histories and scholarship also includes women's absence from the long history of post-Renaissance science and social theory which has taken *man* as its object, either excluding women as unworthy of attention or, more recently, claiming to speak for women as well as men in an allegedly ungendered humanism. Feminists often argue that this work and the theory which informs it has little or nothing to say to women, and in radical-feminist theory it is seen as a way of denying women access to their true selves.[3]

The problems of the relationship between experience and theory, access to knowledge and the patriarchal structure and content of knowledge are of central importance to feminism. To dismiss all theory as an elitist attempt to tell women what their experience really means is not helpful, but it does serve as a reminder of the importance of making theory accessible and of the political importance of transforming the material conditions of knowledge production and women's access to knowledge. It is arguable that a feminist transformation of both knowledge and access to knowledge would enable all feminists to see the relevance and inescapability of theory. It is the argument of this book that rather than turning our backs on theory and taking refuge in experience alone, we should think in terms of transforming both the social relations of knowledge production and the type of knowledge produced. To do so requires that we tackle the fundamental questions of how and where knowledge is produced and by whom, and of what counts as knowledge. It also requires a transformation of the structures which determine how knowledge is disseminated or otherwise.

In addressing questions of the production and distribution of knowledge and developing new stategies which would better serve feminist interests, it is important to keep in mind the relation between experience and knowledge. This relation has been theorized in various ways within the Women's Liberation Movement. None the less, many feminists assume that women's experience, unmediated by further theory, is the source of true knowledge and the basis for feminist politics. This belief rests on the liberal-humanist assumption that subjectivity is the coherent, authentic source of the interpretation of the meaning of 'reality'. Yet whereas the humanist tradition suggests that rationality and modes of scientific thinking common to different individuals, or the artistic perception which is the special gift of the few, give access to a *true* reality, feminists take a different view. For humanist feminists different realities exist for different individuals, all of which are valid, and women's realities differ from those of men. Yet if women's experience is different from the experience of men, it is important to understand why. Either we can see women as essentially different from men or as socially constituted as different and subject to social relations and processes in different ways to men.

While not denying the personal and political importance of experience, it is a central task of this book to argue that it is not enough to refer unproblematically to experience, why we need a theory of the relationship between experience, social power and resistance and what sort of theory can serve us best. For a theoretical perspective to be politically useful to feminists, it should be able to recognize the importance of the *subjective* in constituting the meaning of women's lived reality. It should not deny subjective experience, since the ways in which people make sense of their lives is a necessary starting point for understanding how power relations structure society. Theory must be able to address women's experience by showing where it comes from and how it relates to material social practices and the power relations which structure them. It must be able to recognize and account for competing subjective realities and demonstrate the social interests on behalf of which they work. This involves understanding how particular social structures and processes create the conditions of existence which are at one and the same time both material and discursive. In this process new modes of subjectivity become available, offering the individual both a perspective and a choice, and opening up the possibility of political change. Yet theory must also be able to account for resistance to change. This requires a theory which can encompass differences in subjectivity and different degrees of coherence between subject positions, from, for example, institutional attempts to impose and monitor an all encompassing perspective, as in Catholicism, to subjectivity as the unsystematized accumulation of 'common-sense' knowledge.

While the anti-theoretical tendency within the Women's Liberation Movement rejects all theory as patriarchal and oppressive, there are forms of radical feminism which attack existing social theory and knowledge as patriarchal, yet attempt to develop alternatives. In both American and French radical-feminist theory, language is central. Mary Daly, for example, undertakes a radical deconstruction of patriarchal language and attempts to construct a new feminist discourse in which words acquire new meanings which validate and celebrate a new, positive version of women and our oppression by and resistance to patriarchy. In rewriting the meaning of the feminine or of 'femaleness', feminists make language the site of a struggle over meaning which is a prerequisite for political change. The form which this political change might take depends, in part, on how we reconstitute the meaning of femininity and biological sexual difference. Much French feminist writing, for example, which attacks traditional theory as a pillar of patriarchy and locates language as the site of political struggle, does so in the context of a psychoanalytic theory of meaning. This is most apparent in the work of French feminists who have taken as their starting point Jacques Lacan's psychoanalytic theory of language and subjectivity, for example, Julia Kristeva, Luce Irigaray, and Hélène Cixous. Their work aligns rationality with the masculine and sees the feminine in forms and aspects of language marginalized or suppressed by rationalism: poetic language and the languages of mysticism, madness and magic.[4] Like American radical feminism, French radical theory celebrates female figures, for example witches, who are seen as resisting patriarchy and the rationality through which it exercises its power. The political implications of these rewritings of the feminine require careful consideration and will be discussed in detail later in this book.

The detailed discussion of the positive aspects and problems of attempts to develop new non-patriarchal theories in the chapters which follow inevitably comes from a particular perspective. This is informed by my belief that while we need to develop feminist theory and a concept of feminist rationality, which is different from the rationality of patriarchy, and which no longer dismisses feminine qualities as they are currently defined as irrelevant and inferior, we cannot afford to abandon reason entirely to the interests of patriarchy. Reason, like experience, requires both deconstruction and reconstruction in the interests of feminism.

The task of this book is quite specific. It is to make a case for recent poststructuralist developments in the theory of language, subjectivity and power for knowledge production which will serve feminist interests. It does not claim that a poststructuralist perspective can answer every question which feminists wish to ask, but that poststructuralism offers a useful, productive framework for understanding the mechanisms of power in our society and the possibilities of change.

As a project which seeks to address feminist interests, this book must necessarily confront the question of whose interests feminism represents. The simple answer is that it represents the interests of women. But this is too simple unless we believe in an essential womanhood, common to all women, suppressed or repressed by patriarchy. One problem with the idea of essential womanhood is that it could only surface in a pure form outside of the structures of patriarchy. Another is that the structures of patriarchy are not independent of other forms of power relation, race and class, which are not reducible to each other. There are both theoretical and political objections to essential womanhood which will be made in the course of this book. For the moment, suffice it to say that an adequate feminist politics, and the theory by means of which we formulate it, must take class and race into account, and must be accountable to the oppressed interests which divide women as well as those which all women share. These requirements are guiding principles for an adequate feminist politics. Its details cannot be specified in advance since the precise configuration of power relations in any situation will determine how best we can act.

It is not the purpose of this book to come up with a definitive feminist theory – a totalizing theory of patriarchy. Such a project would have to appeal to some guarantee of its truth, perhaps an essential femininity, which would be set aside from historical process and change. The project of the book is to hold on to feminism as a politics which must needs have tangible results, and to mobilize theory in order to develop strategies for change on behalf of feminist interests. Theory itself is constantly in process, and the argument of this book is focused on the theories which at this moment seem to me to have the power to explain the patriarchal structures within which we live, and our position as women and men within them. The political aim is to change them. It is on this basis that a case will be made for poststructuralist theories of language, subjectivity and power. Chapter 2 begins this task by offering an introductory exposition of the key features of poststructuralist theory.

2

Principles of Poststructuralism

The analysis of the patriarchal structures of society and the positions that we occupy within them requires a theory which can address forms of social organization and the social meanings and values which guarantee or contest them. Yet it must also be able to theorize individual consciousness. We need a theory of the relation between language, subjectivity, social organization and power. We need to understand why women tolerate social relations which subordinate their interests to those of men and the mechanisms whereby women and men adopt particular discursive positions as representative of their interests. This is the agenda which a feminist poststructuralism might consider.

Many theoretical and political influences have helped constitute current poststructuralist theory. Not least among them has been the political agenda of the Women's Liberation Movement. This is the case both for feminists and for many non-feminists whose positions have, in part, been shaped by a hostile relation to feminism. Feminist interests have placed subjectivity, signifying practices and sexuality on the theoretical agenda and focused attention on the political implications of many of the theories which have formed current poststructuralist perspectives. Signifying practices consist of signs, which are ways of communicating meaning and are open to plural interpretations. Particular interpretations have specific social implications, for example, visual signs of femininity, like dress, may imply particular gender roles. The theories which have helped produce poststructuralism include the structural linguistics of Ferdinand de Saussure and Emile Benveniste, Marxism, particularly Louis Althusser's theory of ideology, and the psychoanalysis of Sigmund Freud and Jacques Lacan. They also include Jacques Derrida's theory of 'différance', with its critique of the metaphysics of presence, in which the speaking subject's intention guarantees meaning, and language is a tool for expressing something beyond it, the deconstruction based on Derrida's theory and Michel Foucault's theory of discourse and power.

It is no coincidence that these theorists are all men; this is a consequence of the gender relations which have structured women's absence from the active production of most theory within a whole range of discourses over the last 300 years. It is also a mark of the particular conditions under which prestigious and powerful bodies of knowledge were and are produced. This is manifest in the professional institutions of science, social science, medicine and the humanities which exclude alternative forms of knowledge, in particular those produced by women under different social conditions of knowledge production. Examples include the medical knowledge produced by wise women and midwives in the past and self-help groups now.[1] The fact that most theory has been produced, until recently, by men has not been without its effects on the status of theoretical writing among feminists. It has helped fire the move to reject theory as inherently patriarchal. This tendency has been given impetus by the impenetrability of many important texts for women without privileged access to higher education and by the fact that most of the theorists who have produced poststructuralist texts are themselves unsympathetic to feminism. However it is important to distinguish between the political potential and usefulness of a theory and the particular affiliations of its author. If Foucault's theory of discourse and power can produce in feminist hands an analysis of patriarchal power relations which enables the development of active strategies for change, then it is of little importance whether his own historical analyses fall short of this.

The last fifteen years have seen the beginnings of a radical shift in the degree to which women are represented in knowledge production and in the production of theory both inside and outside official education and research. The growth of consciousness-raising and of self-help and campaign groups around women's issues has begun a process of challenging on the one hand what constitutes useful knowledge and on the other access to knowledge as it is already constituted. These are key political issues, since knowledge brings with it the possibility of power and control. For example, women are increasingly able to question the assumptions underlying dominant gynaecological and obstetric practices and their implications for how we live our lives. This was manifest, for example, in the broad public support among women for the obstetrician, Dr Wendy Savage, in the recent attempt to discipine her for her policy of allowing women to participate in decisions about how to give birth, with or without medical intervention. Within the official institutions of science and research, feminists have begun to challenge the boundaries of existing knowledge, the questions which it asks and answers and its patriarchal implications. Yet challenge from within the structures of the institutions is fraught with contradictions. Many feminists are subject to the dangers of co-option and the reproduction of knowledge as power *over* rather than *for* most women. Feminists within academic institutions concerned with the production of forms of knowledge relevant to the concerns of women, which contribute to the development of practical strategies for change, face difficult but important work.

The political issues which the Women's Liberation Movement has defined as central to the oppression of women include the sexual division of labour, control of sexuality and the relations of reproduction, access to education, jobs and power over our lives. These issues set an agenda for feminist analysis which should produce strategies for change. Feminist theory to date has responded in a range of ways to this political agenda, as can be seen, for example, in feminist approaches to the family. Just think for a moment of the dominant image of the family which confronts us in adverts, magazines, the cinema, television and family portraits, from the royals to our own photo albums. What we see are units of fathers, mothers and children from one or more generations, smiling happily at the camera. In advertising, for example, where images of the family are employed to sell commodities which we are implicitly told will keep our families happy, the composition of the pictures is consistently classically patriarchal. Look for instance at plate 1. At the back of the picture, rising slightly above his wife and children, is the father,

PLATE 1 Patriarchy at its most seductive. *Reproduced by permission of Intersport Great Britain Limited.*

who symbolically encompasses, protects and controls his family. The son is invested with the promise of his father's power by his position directly in front of his father who confronts the camera straight on. The wife is positioned sideways to the camera. Her body faces inwards towards her family. She holds her daughter closely on her knee in a posture which is as traditionally motherly as the father is fatherly. Patriarchal this image may be, but it is immensely seductive. It signifies warmth, happiness and emotional and material security, and every year, despite their experience of the families in which they were children, and the much publicized evidence of the break-up of families in Britain today, thousands of women willingly set out to create conventional family life.

How does feminist theory account for this? Liberal feminism does not offer a radical critique of the family. It takes the basic structure of the nuclear family for granted. Liberal feminists argue that family life and the decision to have children should result from free, individual choice and those who choose to have children should be responsible for them. They stress women's rights as individuals to choice and self-determination, irrespective of biological sex, and their key political objectives are to create the material conditions necessary to ensure woman's self-determination, given her role as mother and primary childcarer. Yet while families may be natural, the sexual division of labour is not. Liberal feminists argue that domestic labour and childcare offer little scope for self-development and self-realization. This is due to the nature of domestic labour, women's economic dependency and their lack of choice in the sexual division of labour. The answer to these problems is seen to lie in the professionalization of domestic labour and childcare on a commercial basis. It is assumed that those who undertake such work for payment do so on the basis of individual, free choice. Such services should be paid for by the consumer with the safety net of state provisions for those unable to afford them. The creation of the material conditions for women's full equality with men should lead eventually to the abolition of the sexual division of labour and ultimately to an androgynous society in which feminine and masculine qualities would be shared by all.

No distinctions between individuals would be made on the basis of biological sex. They would be the result of individual free choice.[2]

In radical-feminist theory, where the biologically based subordination of women is seen as the fundamental form of oppression, prior to class or race, there is no room for the family as it currently exists. Patriarchy is seen as a trans-historical, all-embracing structure, which necessitates women's withdrawal into a separatism from which to develop a new women's culture independent of men. The family is identified as the key instrument in the oppression of women through sexual slavery and forced motherhood. The central political issue for radical feminism is for women to reclaim from men control of their own bodies.

In contrast to liberal feminism, radical feminism does not ignore women's biology. Radical feminists tend to see the root of women's oppression in either women's biological capacity for motherhood or innate, biologically determined male aggression, as manifest in rape, which makes men dangerously different from women. The stress laid on biological sexual difference as the basis of women's oppression under patriarchy leads radical feminists to posit an essential femaleness which women must seek to recapture beyond the structures of the patriarchal family. This true femaleness is linked both to lesbian sexuality and to mothering. Radical-feminist celebrations of women's capacity for motherhood stress its special life-giving qualities which men are said to lack and link women's procreative abilities to psychological qualities which are seen as universally female rather than specific to contemporary patriarchal society. Yet these qualities can only be realized beyond the structures of male control of female sexuality and procreative power.

Socialist feminism has attempted to extend to women the Marxist assumption that human nature is not essential, but socially produced and changing. Socialist feminists do not see patriarchy as monolithic, but as forms of oppression which vary historically. They do not prioritize the oppressive structures of capitalism, patriarchy and racism, but see them as discrete forms of oppression which are often interrelated, as in the case of the family. Socialist feminists stress the need to take account of biology but to see its meaning as historical and social. They do not see women as primarily either sexual or procreative beings – these are only two aspects among many which constitute women. Socialist-feminist analyses stress the need to take account of the psychic dimension of gender, but to see it as historically produced and argue that while the family is a key site of all these issues, it cannot be seen in isolation from broader social relations of work, leisure and public life, all of which require transformation.

Socialist-feminist objectives have profound implications for family life. They include the elimination of the sexual division of labour and the full participation of men in child-rearing; reproductive freedom for women, that is, the right to decide if and when to have children and under what conditions, together with the provision of the conditions necessary for the realization of the right of women to make these choices; the abolition of the privileging of heterosexuality, freedom to define ones own sexuality and the right of lesbians to raise children; the eventual abolition of the categories 'woman' and 'man', and the opening up of all social ways of being to all people.[3]

Whereas the assumptions of liberal and radical feminism about femaleness and femininity are relatively clear-cut, this is not the case in socialist feminism. For liberalism, femaleness and femininity do not determine individual subjectivity. For radical feminism, particular historically specific definitions of womanhood are defined as the essence of what it is to be a woman. In socialist feminism, with its stress on the social construction of femininity, history and change, the particular ways in which gender is constructed and social power exercised cannot be specified in advance by the appeal to some general theory. This recognition of the need for historical specificity does not, however, solve the problem of what theories socialist feminists can most usefully use, and approaches to date have varied from appropriations of Marxist sociology to psychoanalysis.[4]

Liberal, radical and socialist feminism are all critical of the family to varying degrees, but none of them can really account for its appeal. In order to understand why women so willingly take on the role of wife and mother, we need a theory of the relationship between subjectivity and meaning, meaning and social value, the range of possible *normal* subject positions open to women, and the power and powerlessness invested in them. The family, for example, most obviously offers power to men, who might have none outside it. But the positions of wife and mother, though subject to male control, also offer forms of power – the power to socialize children, to run the house and to be the power behind the throne. It is to the understanding of these issues that poststructuralism can usefully contribute.

Liberal, radical and socialist feminist theories developed in the context of existing accounts of social relations. Feminism has taken the dual paths of appropriating existing theories to its needs and of attempting to develop radical alternative theories. Both in the appropriation of existing theory and the development of new theories, feminists require criteria of adequacy which might usefully focus on the basic assumptions, the degree of explanatory power and the political implications which a particular type of analysis yields. It is with these criteria in mind that I would argue the appropriateness of poststructuralism to feminist concerns, not as the answer to *all* feminist questions but as a way of conceptualizing the relationship between language, social institutions and individual consciousness which focuses on how power is exercised and on the possibilities of change.

Poststructuralist Theory

The term 'poststructuralist' is, like all language, plural. It does not have one fixed meaning but is generally applied to a range of theoretical positions developed in and from the work of Derrida (1973, 1976), Lacan (1977), Kristeva (1981, 1984, 1986), Althusser (1971) and Foucault (1978, 1979a and b, 1981, 1986). The work which these theories inform varies considerably. It includes, for example, the apparently 'apolitical' deconstructive criticism, practised by American literary critics in which they are concerned with the 'free play' of meaning in literary texts, the radical-feminist rewriting of the meanings of gender and language in the work of some French feminist writers and the detailed historical analysis of discourse and power in the work of Foucault. The differences between forms of poststructuralism are important. Not all forms are necessarily productive for feminism. In the course of this book, an attempt is made to distinguish between types of poststructuralism and to focus on the particular poststructuralist theories which seem most useful. In doing this I am producing a specific version of poststructuralism which I call 'feminist poststructuralism'. I do so not because I wish to discredit feminist work which uses other forms of poststructuralism, for example, the deconstructive work of Gayatri Spivak,[5] but in order to articulate for the reader a particular position and method which I hold to be useful for feminist practice. In this context, a theory is useful if it is able to address the questions of how social power is exercised and how social relations of gender, class and race might be transformed. This implies a concern with history, absent from many poststructuralist perspectives but central to the work of Michel Foucault.

While different forms of poststructuralism vary both in their practice and in their political implications, they share certain fundamental assumptions about language, meaning and subjectivity. There will be questions which feminists wish to ask which are not compatible with these assumptions, which do not fit into a poststructuralist perspective but require other discursive frameworks. This is the case with many of the concerns of liberal and radical feminism. The least that a feminist poststructuralism can do is explain the assumptions underlying the questions asked and answered by other forms of feminist theory, making their political assumptions explicit. Poststructuralism can also indicate the types of discourse from which particular feminist questions come and locate them both socially and institutionally. Most important of all, it can explain the implications for feminism of these other discourses.

In the rest of this chapter, a brief account is given of the key features of poststructuralist theory. While some attention is paid to differences between forms of poststructuralism, the main emphasis is on producing a form of poststructuralism which can meet feminist needs. This chapter is an initial introduction to the theory which is explored, expanded and clarified in the rest of the book. The theoretical material involved is not easy, but I hope that by the end of the book the reader will have been offered a useful understanding of the relationship between poststructuralist theory and feminist practice.

Language

For poststructuralist theory the common factor in the analysis of social organization, social meanings, power and individual consciousness is *language*. Language is the place where actual and possible forms of social organization and their likely social and political consequences are defined and contested. Yet it is also the place where our sense of ourselves, our subjectivity, is *constructed*. The assumption that subjectivity is constructed implies that it is not innate, not genetically determined, but socially produced. Subjectivity is produced in a whole range of discursive practices – economic, social and political – the meanings of which are a constant site of struggle over power. Language is not the expression of unique individuality; it constructs the individual's subjectivity in ways which are socially specific. Moreover for poststructuralism, subjectivity is neither unified nor fixed. Unlike humanism, which implies a conscious, knowing, unified, rational subject, poststructuralism theorizes subjectivity as a site of disunity and conflict, central to the process of political change and to preserving the status quo. For example, in the events on the picket lines during the 1984–5 miners' strike in Britain, the fundamental conflict of interests involved led to a situation in which the actions of trade unionists, politicians and the police were given radically different meanings by various interest groups. These different meanings, which revolved around questions of legality and morality, produced conflicting subject positions for the individuals involved. The miners were simultaneously criminal thugs and ordinary decent men, anxious to protect their livelihoods and communities; the police were both upholders of the law and agents of class interest from which all vestiges of morality and decency had disappeared. The need to rescue a coherent subjectivity from this battle over the meaning of the strike led to a hardening of positions between striking and working miners, the police and the politicians which precluded any shift in power relations through the realignment of interests.

Like all theories, poststructuralism makes certain assumptions about language, subjectivity, knowledge and truth. Its founding insight, taken from the structuralist linguistics of Ferdinand de Saussure, is that language, far from reflecting an already given social reality, constitutes social reality for us. Neither social reality nor the 'natural' world has fixed intrinsic meanings which language reflects or expresses. Different languages and different discourses within the same language divide up the world and give it meaning in different ways which cannot be reduced to one another through translation or by an appeal to universally shared concepts reflecting a fixed reality. For example, the meanings of femininity and masculinity vary from culture to culture and language to language. They even vary between discourses within a particular language, between different feminist discourses, for instance, and are subject to historical change, from Victorian values to the suffrage movement, for example.

All forms of poststructuralism assume that meaning is constituted within language and is not guaranteed by the subject which speaks it. In this sense all poststructuralism is post-Saussurean. While there can be no essential qualities of femininity or masculinity, given for all times and reflected in language and the social relations which language structures, different forms of poststructuralism theorize the production of meaning in different ways. Psychoanalytic forms of poststructuralism look to a fixed psycho-sexual order; deconstruction looks to the relationship between different texts; and Foucauldian theory, which is arguably of most interest to feminists, looks to historically specific discursive relations and social practices. While each of these approaches is explained in the course of this book the main focus is on the latter approach.

In this theory the meaning of gender is both socially produced and variable between different forms of discourse. Pornography and much advertising, for example, offer us models of femininity in which a particular version of female sexuality is paramount. It is a form of femininity in which women direct themselves totally to the satisfaction of the male gaze, male fantasies and male desires and gain an arguably masochistic pleasure in doing so. This contrasts with other versions of femininity, which stress women's asexuality, exalting either virginity or motherhood, and which call for different sorts of masochistic feminine behaviour.

An understanding of Saussure's theory of the 'sign' is fundamental to all poststructuralism. It is Saussure's insistence on a pre-given fixed structuring of language, prior to its realization in speech or writing, which earns his linguistics the title 'structural'. Saussure theorized language as an abstract system, consisting of chains of signs. Each sign is made up of a *signifier* (sound or written image) and a *signified* (meaning). The two components of the sign are related to each other in an arbitrary way and there is therefore no natural connection between the sound image and the concept it identifies. The meaning of signs is not intrinsic but relational. Each sign derives its meaning from its difference from all the other signs in the language chain. It is not anything intrinsic to the signifier 'whore', for example, that gives it its meaning, but rather its difference from other signifiers of womanhood such as 'virgin' and 'mother'.

Poststructuralism, while building on Saussure's theory, radically modifies and transforms some of its important aspects. It takes from Saussure the principle that meaning is produced within language rather than reflected by language, and that individual signs do not have intrinsic meaning but acquire meaning through the language chain and their difference within it from other signs. These principles are important because they make language truly social and a site of political struggle. If we take the example of 'woman', Saussure's theory implies that the meaning of 'woman', or the qualities identified as womanly, are not fixed by a natural world and reflected in the term 'woman', but socially produced within language, plural and subject to change. Yet, to satisfy feminist interests, we need to move beyond Saussure's theory of an abstract system of language. To gain the full benefit of Saussure's theory of meaning, we need to view language as a system always existing in historically specific discourses. Once language is understood in terms of competing discourses, competing ways of giving meaning to the world, which imply differences in the organization of social power, then language becomes an important site of political struggle. This point will be illustrated in greater detail in chapters 4 and 5, which look at the relationship between subjectivity, discourse and power.

The poststructuralist move beyond Saussure involves a critique of the fixing of meaning in the Saussurean sign through the arbitrary coming together of the signifiers and signifieds to form *positive* terms. Saussure attempts to locate meaning in the language system itself but then sees it as single, as 'fixed':

> A linguistic system is a series of differences of sound combined with differences of ideas, but the pairing of a certain number of acoustical signs with as many cuts made from the mass of thought engenders a system of values, and this system serves as the effective link between the phonic and the psychological elements within each sign. Although both the signified and the signifier are purely differential and negative when considered separately, their combination is a positive fact. (Saussure, 1974, p. 120)

The problem with this theory is that it does not account for the plurality of meaning or changes in meaning. It cannot account for why the signifier 'woman' can have many conflicting meanings which change over time. For Saussure, signs are fixed as positive facts which are the product of the conventions of a 'speech community' (1974, p. 14). Language does not originate from individual, intentional subjects and the individual's relation to language is 'largely unconscious' (1974, p. 72). Yet the language which the individual acquires consists of fixed meanings which are the result of an already existing social contract to which individual speakers are subject. The poststructuralist answer to the problems of the plurality of meaning and change is to question the location of social meaning in fixed signs. It speaks instead of signifiers in which the signified is never fixed once and for all, but is constantly *deferred*.

It is in the work of Jacques Derrida that this critique of the Saussurean sign is made most clearly.[6] Derrida questions Saussure's *logocentrism* in which signs have an already fixed meaning recognized by the self-consciousness of the rational speaking subject. Derrida moves from the Saussurean focus on speech to a concern with writing and textuality and replaces the fixed signifieds of Saussure's chains of signs with a concept of *différance* in which meaning is produced via the dual strategies of difference and deferral. For Derrida there can be no fixed signifieds (concepts), and signifiers (sound or written images), which have identity only in their difference from one another, are subject to an endless process of deferral. The effect of representation, in which meaning is apparently fixed, is but a temporary retrospective fixing. Signifiers are always located in a discursive context and the temporary fixing of meaning in a specific reading of a signifier depends on this discursive context. The meaning of the signifier 'woman' varies from ideal to victim to object of sexual desire, according to its context. Consequently, it is always open to challenge and redefinition with shifts in its discursive context. What it means at any particular moment depends on the discursive relations within which it is located, and it is open to constant rereading and reinterpretation. Deconstruction theorizes the discursive context as the relationship of difference between written texts, and while insisting that non-discursive forces are important, does not spell out the social power relations within which texts are located. However, a feminist poststructuralism must pay full attention to the social and institutional context of textuality in order to address the power relations of everyday life. Social meanings are produced within social institutions and practices in which individuals, who are shaped by these institutions, are agents of change, rather than its authors, change which may either serve hegemonic interests or challenge existing power relations.

Language, in the form of an historically specific range of ways of giving meaning to social reality, offers us various discursive positions, including modes of femininity and masculinity, through which we can consciously live our lives. A glance at women's magazines, for example, reveals a range of often competing subject positions offered to women readers, from career woman to romantic heroine, from successful wife and mother to irresistible sexual object. These different positions which magazines construct in their various features, advertising and fiction are part of the battle to determine the day to day practices of family life, education, work and leisure. How women understand the sexual division of labour, for example, whether in the home or in paid work, is crucial to its maintenance or transformation. Discourses of femininity and masculinity bear centrally on this understanding and it is in this sense that language in the form of various discourses is, in Louis Althusser's terms, the place in which we represent to ourselves our 'lived relation' to our material conditions of existence (Althusser, 1971).[7]

How we live our lives as conscious thinking subjects, and how we give meaning to the material social relations under which we live and which structure our everyday lives, depends on the range and social power of existing discourses, our access to them and the political strength of the interests which they represent. For example, there are currently several conflicting accounts of the sexual division of labour which inform different common-sense assumptions about women's subjectivity and social role. These include versions which see it as natural because biologically determined, as, for example in sociobiology and behaviourist psychology, and theories which see it as a socially produced structure, as in much sociological theory. Marxists understand it to be an effect of capitalism, while socialist feminists see it as intrinsic to the capitalist mode of production but not reducible to it. Alternatively, radical feminism sees the sexual division of labour as an effect of patriarchy, the causes of which tend to be located in the nature or structure of masculinity.

Each of these accounts is competing for the meaning of a plural signifier, the sexual division of labour, in ways which imply not only different social and political consequences for women, but also the different forms of feminine subjectivity which are the precondition for meaningful action. Biologically based theory, for example, and the common-sense positions which it informs, offer women forms of fixed subjectivity which render the status quo natural and marginalize attempts to change it as unnatural. Conversely, in radical-feminist biologism, the status quo is rejected as an unnatural, patriarchal distortion of the truly female, in favour of a separate women's culture based in women's biological nature, but defined in different, more positive ways.

Marxism and Poststructuralism

As a theory of social meaning and power, poststructuralist work on discourse in its social and historical context has developed in a relation of difference from Marxism. A feminist poststructuralism might well look to Marxism for various aspects of its theory of language and subjectivity. In the development of Western political philosophy, the writings of Marx marked a crucial break with the assumptions of liberalism, the dominant position, not just about political economy but about consciousness and language. In a reversal of liberal priorities, early Marxist writing decentred the sovereign, rational humanist consciousness of liberal political philosophy and economics, making consciousness not the origin of social relations but their effect. As such, consciousness is always historically and culturally specific. Moreover, Marxism argues that all class societies produce a range of competing and conflicting forms of consciousness. In capitalist society different ways of thinking represent competing class interests, determined ultimately by the conflict of interests between labour and capital.[8]

 It is the Marxist linking of ideology with material interests and its integral role in the reproduction of specific forms of power relations in society which is important for feminism. The ways in which individuals understand their material conditions of existence becomes a site of struggle where they can either be reproduced or transformed. For example, under capitalism, as Marx theorized it, the mass of the working population are forced to sell their ability to work, their labour power, to those who have the means to produce goods and services, the owners of capital. In this process the owners of capital make profit through the *surplus value* produced by the workforce. This is that part of the value of the products which surpasses the cost of materials, machinery and labour power. Profit is made by paying labour less than the value which it produces. The worker has no alternative than to work for as little as the employer pays her. Yet, in the dominant liberal discourses of capitalist society, this oppressive relationship between capital and labour is represented as a free contract between rational, sovereign individuals. From the perspective of how individual workers and employers understand their lives, this interpretation may have all the force, for them, of lived experience.

However, experience for Marxism as for poststructuralism, is a linguistic construct. The dominant liberal account of the experience of capitalist relations of production is one way among others of interpreting the world and, for Marxism, a false one which helps reproduce oppressive power relations by misrepresenting the real relations of capitalist society. Marxist discourse is able to use the terms 'real' and 'false' because it has a concept of historical materialist *science* which can offer a true explanation of capitalism, guaranteed by the Marxist principle of the ultimate determining power of the relations of production. Poststructuralist discourses reject the claim that scientific theories can give access to truth. As most scientists themselves would acknowledge, it can only ever produce specific knowledge, with particular implications. However, as radical-feminist writers like Mary Daly and Adrienne Rich have demonstrated so clearly, both the sciences and the social sciences often do make claims to objectivity, at the very least in their style of writing, which function as a way of masking assumptions and interests, and of discounting subjective investment.[9] One radical-feminist answer to this problem is to abandon traditional rationality and celebrate irrational forms of discourse and subjectivity. Yet it is not ultimately helpful merely to reverse the rational–irrational opposition. It needs to be thoroughly revised and reconstituted in ways which no longer marginalize women's interests.

In poststructuralist feminism, we can choose between different accounts of reality on the basis of their social implications. It is this question of social implications which has led many feminists to question the Marxist assumption that the economic mode of production is always determinate where the structures of patriarchy are concerned. None the less, socialist feminists have applied Marxist models of ideology to gender relations, attempting to theorize patriarchal ideologies as misrepresentations of the real power relations between the sexes in society. For example, the prevalent belief that women are equal but different, and the sexual division of labour and differential gender characteristics which this theory guarantees, are seen to mask structural relations of inequality which ensure that women are never equal.

Yet while, for Marxism, the economic relations of production are determining in the 'last instance', the ideological realm, structured by the various apparatuses of the state and civil society enjoy, in non-economistic Marxism, a measure of *relative autonomy*. Louis Althusser argues in his influential text 'Ideology and the Ideological State Apparatuses' (1971) that the reproduction of the relations of production, which is central to the maintenance of capitalist social relations, is secured by *ideological state apparatuses* such as schools, the church, the family, the law, the political system, trade unionism, the media and culture, backed by the repressive apparatuses of the police and the armed forces. Each ideological state apparatus contributes to the reproduction of capitalist relations of exploitation in the 'way proper to it' and the means by which it determines dominant meanings is *language*:

> The political apparatus by subjecting individuals to the political State ideology, the 'indirect' (parliamentary) or 'direct' (plebiscitary or fascist) 'democratic' ideology. The communications apparatus by cramming every 'citizen' with daily doses of nationalism, chauvinism, liberalism, moralism, etc., by means of the press, the radio and television. The same goes for the cultural apparatus (the role of sport in chauvanism is of the first importance), etc. The religious apparatus by recalling in sermons and the

other great ceremonies of Birth, Marriage and Death, that man is only ashes, unless he loves his neighbour to the extent of turning the other cheek to whoever strikes first. The family apparatus . . . but there is no need to go on. (Althusser, 1971, p. 146)

Language, in the form of what Althusser calls 'ideology in general', is the means by which individuals are governed by the ideological state apparatuses in the interests of the ruling class (gender, or racial group). The way in which ideology functions for the individual, according to Althusser, is by *interpellating* her as a subject, that is, constituting her subjectivity for her in language. Whereas subjectivity appears obvious to the individual, it is an effect of ideology:

> Like all obviousnesses, including those that make a word 'name a thing' or 'have a meaning' (therefore including the obviousness of the 'transparency' of language), the obviousness that you and I are subjects – and that that does not cause any problems – is an ideological effect, the elementary ideological effect. (p. 161)

Althusser argues that the interpellation of individuals as subjects is a structural feature of all ideology:

> I shall then suggest that ideology 'acts' or 'functions' in such a way that it 'recruits' subjects among the individuals (it recruits them all), or 'transforms' the individuals into subjects (it transforms them all) by that very precise operation which I have called *interpellation* or hailing, and which can be imagined along the lines of the most commonplace everyday police (or other) hailing: 'Hey, you there!' (pp. 162–3)

This process relies on a structure of recognition by the individual of herself as the subject of ideology which is also a process of misrecognition. It is misrecognition in the sense that the individual, on assuming the position of subject in ideology, assumes that she is the *author* of the ideology which constructs her subjectivity.

The process of the interpellation of individuals as subjects through which they become the agents of specific ideologies, sustaining particular material social relations, relies on a theory of 'ideology in general' which, in poststructuralism, is a theory of language in general. It assumes that ideology is always the precondition of social existence which takes place through historically specific ideolog*ies*. Ideology mediates between individuals and their real conditions of existence, much as language does in post-Saussurean theory. It functions by interpellating individuals as subjects within specific ideologies which exist in material apparatuses and their practices. Similarly, in poststructuralist theory, the structure and function of the position of the subject within discourse is the precondition for the individual to assume historically specific forms of subjectivity within particular discourses. In Althusser's formulation, the relationship between the individual and the subject position which she or he takes up in a specific ideology is *imaginary*. To understand the force of this term, we need to look at the Lacanian psychoanalysis, from which it is taken, and which is explained in chapter 3. The crucial point for the moment is that in taking on a subject position, the individual assumes that she is the author of the ideology or discourse which she is speaking. She speaks or thinks as if she were in control of meaning. She 'imagines' that she is indeed the type of subject which humanism proposes – rational, unified, the source rather than the effect of language. It is the imaginary quality of the individual's identification with a subject position which gives it so much psychological and emotional force.

The feminist poststructuralism for which this book is arguing takes much from Marxist discourse, particularly Althusserian Marxism: for example, the material nature of ideology, or in poststructuralist terms, discourse, the importance of economic relations of production, the class structure of society and the integral relationship between theory and practice. However, it does not assume in advance that discourses and the forms of social power which they legitimize are necessarily ultimately reducible to the capital–labour relationship, even in the last instance. In any particular historically specific analysis, this may indeed be the case. There is, however, space within this poststructuralism for other forms of power relation, such as gender and race, which must not necessarily be subordinated to class analysis, although questions of class and the interrelation of forms of oppression will often be crucial to the analysis.

Like Althusserian Marxism, feminist poststructuralism makes the primary assumption that it is language which enables us to think, speak and give meaning to the world around us. Meaning and consciousness do not exist outside language. Stated in this way, poststructuralist theory may seem to resemble a range of humanist discourses which take consciousness and language as the fundamental human attributes. Yet in all poststructuralist discourses, subjectivity and rational consciousness are themselves put into question. We are neither the authors of the ways in which we understand our lives, nor are we unified rational beings. For feminist poststructuralism, it is language in the form of conflicting discourses which constitutes us as conscious thinking subjects and enables us to give meaning to the world and to act to transform it.

Subjectivity

The terms *subject* and *subjectivity* are central to poststructuralist theory and they mark a crucial break with humanist conceptions of the individual which are still central to Western philosophy and political and social organization. 'Subjectivity' is used to refer to the conscious and unconscious thoughts and emotions of the individual, her sense of herself and her ways of understanding her relation to the world. Humanist discourses presuppose an essence at the heart of the individual which is unique, fixed and coherent and which makes her what she *is*. The nature of this essence varies between different forms of humanist discourse. It may be the unified rational consciousness of liberal political philosophy, the essence of womanhood at the heart of much radical-feminist discourse or the true human nature, alienated by capitalism, which is the focus of humanist Marxism. Against this irreducible humanist essence of subjectivity, poststructuralism proposes a subjectivity which is precarious, contradictory and in process, constantly being reconstituted in discourse each time we think or speak.

The political significance of decentring the subject and abandoning the belief in essential subjectivity is that it opens up subjectivity to change. In making our subjectivity the product of the society and culture within which we live, feminist poststructuralism insists that forms of subjectivity are produced historically and change with shifts in the wide range of discursive fields which constitute them. However, feminist poststructuralism goes further than this to insist that the individual is always the site of conflicting forms of subjectivity. As we acquire language, we learn to give voice – meaning – to our experience and to understand it according to particular ways of thinking, particular discourses, which pre-date our entry into language. These ways of thinking constitute our consciousness, and the positions with which we identify structure our sense of ourselves, our subjectivity. Having grown up within a particular system of meanings and values, which may well be contradictory, we may find ourselves resisting alternatives. Or, as we move out of familiar circles, through education or politics, for example, we may be exposed to alternative ways of constituting the meaning of our experience which seem to address our interests more directly. For many women this is the meaning of the practice of consciousness-raising developed by the Women's Liberation Movement. The collective discussion of personal problems and conflicts, often previously understood as the result of personal inadequacies and neuroses, leads to a recognition that what have been experienced as personal failings are socially produced conflicts and contradictions shared by many women in similar social positions. This process of discovery can lead to a rewriting of personal experience in terms which give it social, changeable causes.

The inadequacies widely felt by the new mother, for example, who is inserted in a discourse of motherhood in which she is exposed to childcare demands structured by the social relations of the patriarchal nuclear family, may leave her feeling an unnatural or bad parent. As mother she is supposed to meet all the child's needs single-handed, to care for and stimulate the child's physical, emotional and mental development and to feel fulfilled in doing so. The recognition that feelings of inadequacy or failure are common among women in similar positions, that the current organization of childcare is the result, not of nature, but of social and historical developments in the organization of work and procreation, and that contemporary definitions of woman as mother conflict with other subject positions which we are encouraged to assume, offers the frustrated mother a new subject position from which to make sense of her situation, a position which makes her the subject rather than the cause of the contraditions which she is living. As the subject of a range of conflicting discourses, she is *subjected* to their contradictions at great emotional cost.

Poststructuralist feminist theory suggests that experience has no inherent essential meaning. It may be given meaning in language through a range of discursive systems of meaning, which are often contradictory and constitute conflicting versions of social reality, which in turn serve conflicting interests. This range of discourses and their material supports in social institutions and practices is integral to the maintenance and contestation of forms of social power, since social reality has no meaning except in language.

Yet language, in the form of socially and historically specific discourses, cannot have any social and political effectivity except in and through the actions of the individuals who become its bearers by taking up the forms of subjectivity and the meanings and values which it proposes and acting upon them. The individual is both the site for a range of possible forms of subjectivity and, at any particular moment of thought or speech, a subject, subjected to the regime of meaning of a particular discourse and enabled to act accordingly. The position of subject from which language is articulated, from which speech acts, thoughts or writing appear to originate, is integral to the structure of language and, by extension, to the structure of conscious subjectivity which it constitutes. Language and the range of subject positions which it offers always exists in historically specific discourses which inhere in social institutions and practices and can be organized analytically in discursive fields.

Language as Discourse

Social structures and processes are organized through institutions and practices such as the law, the political system, the church, the family, the education system and the media, each of which is located in and structured by a particular *discursive field*. The concept of a discursive field was produced by the French theorist, Michel Foucault, as part of an attempt to understand the relationship between language, social institutions, subjectivity and power. Discursive fields consist of competing ways of giving meaning to the world and of organizing social institutions and processes. They offer the individual a range of modes of subjectivity. Within a discursive field, for instance, that of the law or the family, not all discourses will carry equal weight or power. Some will account for and justify the appropriateness of the status quo. Others will give rise to challenge to existing practices from within or will contest the very basis of current organization and the selective interests which it represents. Such discourses are likely to be marginal to existing practice and dismissed by the hegemonic system of meanings and practices as irrelevant or bad.

In the field of legal discourse in Britain today, for example, the legal apparatuses are not homogeneous in their views on the best way of organizing the system of trial, punishment, compensation and the rehabilitation of offenders. While there are dominant forms of legal practice, informed by particular values and interests, the discourses which justify or contest this practice are manifold. Some professionals and social groups are currently pressing for stronger custodial sentences, others for short, sharp shocks or for capital punishment. In opposition to this there are groups and individuals who champion greater use of community service and fines rather than prison. Certain types of crime, for example against the state, the police and property are defined as worse than others and the hierarchization of crimes will vary between legal discourses and from interest group to interest group.

Yet in any society, one set of legal discourses is dominant and it reflects particular values and class, gender and racial interests. Current legal practice in rape cases in Britain, for example, which claims to represent 'natural justice', can be read as serving the interests of men in reproducing and legitimizing dominant forms of femininity and masculinity. What is in question here is the meaning of the 'natural' in 'natural justice'. Examining and sentencing practices in the courts often endorse a view of rape as a natural extension of an active male sexuality in the face of female 'provocation'. In the view of some judges, this may take the form of going out alone at night, wearing a mini-skirt or being a prostitute.

The values and interests which constitute norms of provocation in the eyes of judges and the police are not specific to the legal apparatuses. They have to be understood in the context of widely held beliefs about female sexuality and women's proper place and lifestyle which cross a whole range of discursive fields from the family, education and employment to the representation of women in the media. These are beliefs in which individuals have vested interests. Dominant discourses of female sexuality, which define it as naturally passive, together with dominant social definitions of women's place as first and foremost in the home, can be found in social policy, medicine, education, the media and the church and elsewhere. The conclusions widely drawn from such assumptions include the belief that women who are not sexually passive or virginally modest in their self-presentation are 'asking for it' and that a woman who goes out after dark should be accompanied by a man – father, brother, husband, boyfriend – who is responsible for her welfare. A common response to the threat of rape, especially on university campuses, is to tell women to stay in after dark. What is at issue is the meaning of the ways in which women dress or how we live. In some rape cases to go out unaccompanied has been interpreted as yet another sign of sexual availability, a provocation to male sexuality. This is itself socially constructed as an ever-present, powerful thrust of sexual drives, which society, and women in particular, must hold in check by not offering 'unreasonable' provocation. Attempts by feminist lawyers and women's pressure groups to change meanings, for example the assumptions about femininity which inform dominant legal practice, constitute a part of the legal discursive field which challenges and seeks to transform the hegemonic discourse from a position of relative powerlessness. The implications of this challenge are extremely important, both for rape victims and for all women.

The differences between competing views of justice within the field of legal discourse are articulated in language and in the material organization of state institutions which control the meaning of justice, punishment, compensation and rehabilitation. Institutions such as the courts, prisons and the probation service define justice in ways which serve particular values and interests. Yet the meaning and political significance of the organization of legal institutions and processes are themselves a site of struggle. They will vary according to the discursive position from which they are interpreted. While agents of the official organs of the state and the legislature may seek to explain and justify the system in terms of a discourse of law and order based on shared 'traditional' values and specific notions of what constitutes crime, others may see the system in radically different terms. It can be seen, for example, as repressive towards particular subordinated interest groups like women or blacks, and the discourses developed to represent these interests will seek among other things to redefine what constitutes crime by taking into account patriarchy and racism, and the social deprivations which they uphold. The redefinition of crimes can have important implications for the forms of subjectivity available to the 'criminal'. She may become a freedom fighter where she was a terrorist or, for example, in the case of attacks on sex shops, a champion of women's interests in the campaign against violence against women, rather than the perpetrator of criminal damage. The meaning of the existing structure of social institutions, as

much as the structures themselves and the subject positions
which they offer their subjects, is a site of political struggle
waged mainly, though not exclusively, in *language*.

Where women are concerned this can be seen very clearly in
conflicting definitions of the true or desirable nature and
function of the family and more specifically what it means to be
a wife and mother. Two examples will help illustrate this point.
In conservative discourse the family is the natural basic unit of
the social order, meeting individual emotional, sexual and
practical needs, and it is primarily responsible for the reproduction and socialization of children. Power relations in the
family, in which men usually have more power than women and
women more power than children, are seen as part of a God-
given natural order which guarantees the sexual division of
labour within the family. The naturalness of women's responsibility for domestic labour and childcare is balanced by the
naturalness of men's involvement in the worlds of work and
politics. Both partners are equal in worth but different. The
organization of society in family units guarantees the reproduction of social values and skills in differential class and gender
terms. To be a wife and mother is seen as women's primary role
and the source of full self-realization. The natural structure of
femininity will ensure that women can achieve fulfilment
through these tasks.

Women's magazines are addressed to the question of how
women might best negotiate their familial roles. Relationships
with men and children, concerns of family life more generally
and the skills needed for a successful career in domesticity are
central to the features, fiction, advertising and advice columns
which constitute the dominant message of the magazines. Yet it
is on the problem pages that the values underpinning the
magazines as a whole become most explicit. The type of advice
given to women on marital problems, in particular, urges
women to make the best of the oppressive structures of family
life. As wives and mothers, we are encouraged to accommodate
ourselves to families at the expense of our own feelings and the
quality of our lives. Examples of this can be found in the advice
columns of all popular women's magazines.

While it would be most effective to let examples of readers' letters and the replies to them speak for themselves, the magazines do not allow the quotation of published letters. The discussion of the example which follows refers to one such real letter from a woman, whom I shall call Penny, whose husband has abused her for years in the context of a relationship where he has all the economic power. The letter describes long years of physical and mental cruelty by the husband which end in the woman's nervous breakdown. Penny describes how a recent change in her husband and an end to domestic violence has left her with feelings of contempt for him together with a desire to break away from a marriage which offers her no emotional satisfaction. She is restrained from doing so by the material constraints of marriage – she has nowhere else to go.

The reply to this letter urges Penny to make the best of her marriage and to work to improve its quality. The agony columnist regrets not the state of the marriage but her correspondent's attitude to it, suggesting it is a pity that after having stayed with her husband when he was 'mean, a bully and a drinker', she should now feel so hostile towards him. The reply argues that contempt inspires contemptibility rather than the other way round and suggests ways in which Penny might improve the quality of her relationship with her husband through demonstrations of affection which the correspondent has stressed she does not feel. Both the letter and the reply assume that language is transparent and expresses a singular reality of experience to which the reader, too, is offered access. The answer to Penny's appeal for advice reinforces the patri- archal values of family life.

The reply exemplifies the way in which conservative discourses fail to take issue with the power relations, particularly the economic ones both within the family and in society at large which keep women trapped. Instead it reproduces and legitimizes these relations by placing the responsibility to improve family relations on Penny, even suggesting that her wrong attitudes are responsible for the current state of relations between Penny and her husband. It offers her only one legitimate subject position, that of a long-suffering patient Griselda. There is no sense of the relationship as an enactment of patriarchal familial oppression and no question of self-determination for the woman involved.

In contrast, radical- and socialist-feminist discourses theorize the family as the instrument *par excellence* of the oppression of women through male control of female sexuality and procreative powers and their control of economic power. The family is seen as the major social instrument which ties women to heterosexual monogamy and constitutes their sexuality masochistically in the interests of the satisfaction of male desire. Instead of it being natural for women to defer constantly to the interests of men and children, feminism sees such behaviour as a result of forms of oppression exercised through the legally, economically and ideologically defined structures of the family and through the internalization of a masochistic form of femininity. Masochistic femininity is also acquired through the family, which encourages women to seek satisfaction in constantly deferring to men and to men's definitions of what they should be. It helps make women psychologically accepting of the material structures of their oppression. Yet the reality of the family as a social institution defined and materially supported by the law, the tax system, the welfare system, education, the media, the churches and a range of other social institutions, together with the lack of a real alternative to the patriarchal nuclear family, means that it is very difficult for women to opt out of family life. New subject positions, imaginable in theory or in feminist futurist novels like *Woman on the Edge of Time* (Piercy, 1979), in which sexual divisions of labour and of personal qualities have been dissolved, require new sets of material relations for their realization. Alternative feminist discourses of 'family' life as found, for example, in the last chapter of *The Anti-social Family* (Barrett and McIntosh, 1982), and the new forms of social organization which they imply are still marginal and powerless in the social hierarchy of those Western societies which they seek to transform.

Feminist poststructuralism, then, is a mode of knowledge production which uses poststructuralist theories of language, subjectivity, social processes and institutions to understand existing power relations and to identify areas and strategies for change. Through a concept of *discourse*, which is seen as a structuring principle of society, in social institutions, modes of thought and individual subjectivity, feminist poststructuralism is able, in detailed, historically specific analysis, to explain the working of power on behalf of specific interests and to analyse the opportunities for resistance to it. It is a theory which decentres the rational, self-present subject of humanism, seeing subjectivity and consciousness, as socially produced in language, as a site of struggle and potential change. Language is not transparent as in humanist discourse, it is not expressive and does not label a 'real' world. Meanings do not exist prior to their articulation in language and language is not an abstract system, but is always socially and historically located in discourses. Discourses represent political interests and in consequence are constantly vying for status and power. The site of this battle for power is the subjectivity of the individual and it is a battle in which the individual is an active but not sovereign protagonist.

At the level of the individual, this theory is able to offer an explanation of where our experience comes from, why it is contradictory or incoherent and why and how it can change. It offers a way of understanding the importance of subjective motivation and the illusion of full subjectivity necessary for individuals to act in the world. It can also account for the political limitations of change at the level of subjective consciousness stressing the importance of the material relations and practices which constitute individuals as embodied subjects with particular but not inevitable forms of conscious and unconscious motivation and desires which are themselves the effect of the social institutions and processes which structure society. It is for these reasons that this particular form of poststructuralism is a productive theory for feminism.

Feminism, in all its forms, and poststructuralism share a concern with subjectivity. The recent feminist movement began with the politics of the personal, challenging the unified, apparently ungendered individual of liberalism and suggesting that, in its gender blindness, liberal humanism masks structures of male privilege and domination. Poststructuralism, too, has been anxious to deconstruct the liberal-humanist subject in order to theorize how meanings are produced, how they are effective, why they conflict and how they change. In both cases the influence of Freud and of more recent psychoanalytic theory has been an important factor, influencing how subjectivity has been thought and what questions it has seemed important to ask and answer. The next chapter turns to the relationship between feminist poststructuralism and psychoanalysis.

3

Feminist Poststructuralism and Psychoanalysis

Since 1970 considerable attention has been paid by feminist theorists to psychoanalytic models of sexuality and subjectivity. Influenced by Freud and by the French psychoanalyst, Jacques Lacan, many feminists have attempted to make psychoanalytic theory the key to understanding the acquisition of gendered subjectivity, either by accepting the terms of Freudian discourse, or by advocating psychoanalytic theory as a way of understanding the structures of femininity and masculinity under patriarchy, together with the social and cultural forms to which these structures give rise. Recent feminist writing has, for example, taken up the Freudian model of psycho-sexual development as a basis for understanding female sexuality, femininity and the representation of women in film, literature and the media.[1]

Psychoanalysis offers a universal theory of the *psychic* construction of gender identity on the basis of repression. In doing so, it gives specific answers to the question of what constitutes subjectivity, how we acquire gendered subjectivity and internalize certain norms and values. It offers a framework from within which femininity and masculinity can be understood and a theory of consciousness, language and meaning. The question which this chapter asks is how useful this framework is from a feminist poststructuralist perspective, particularly in the light of the current popularity which psychoanalytic theory is enjoying in cultural analysis. Psychoanalysis has itself been influential in the development of poststructuralist theory, and it is important to understand this influence, and where and why a feminist poststructuralism needs to take issue with psychoanalysis. In this chapter, I offer a reading of psychoanalytic theories which attempts both to make them accessible and to assess them from the perspective of a feminist poststructuralism.

If psychoanalysis is currently popular with feminists as a way of understanding the construction of sexuality, initial feminist responses to Freud were far from positive. Kate Millett, for example, in her highly influential *Sexual Politics*, first published in 1970, argued that psychoanalysis bore a large measure of responsibility for the sexual counter-revolution of the 1940s and 1950s. While recognizing the need to address 'the socialization processes of temperament and role differentiation' and acknowledging that marriage and family life were fundamental pillars of the patriarchal order, Millett argued against the biologically based psychic structuring of femininity, which she took to be at the centre of Freud's work (Millett, 1977, p. 117). *Sexual Politics* recognized the contradictions in Freud's texts, but chose to focus on his theory of femininity, in which anatomical difference directly affects the structure of the feminine character. This reading emphasized anatomical determinism at the expense of other, arguably more productive, aspects of Freudian theory. Although *Sexual Politics* begins with a carefully argued reading of Freud, it goes on to collapse the feminine into the female and the psychic into the biological, undermining the more progressive aspects of Freudian theory, for example the theory of the unconscious and of language.

A similar critique of Freud was made in 1972 by Shulamith Firestone in *The Dialectic of Sex*. This text points to how the oppression of women has been ideologically reinforced by Freud's fixing of certain norms of femininity as the effects of universal psycho-sexual structures. None the less the identification of femininity under capitalist patriarchy as at least in part passive, masochistic and narcissistic does have some persuasive power. The question which needs addressing is why femininity is like this. Is it useful to see it as an effect of fixed psycho-sexual structures or should we be aiming for a theory which is historically and culturally specific and in which femininity is viewed as changeable? Furthermore we need to consider whether psychoanalysis is either useful or necessary to the production of such a theory.

Freud's Theory of the Acquisition of Gender

Freud's psycho-sexual theory was developed as a way of understanding mentally disturbed patients by positing the pattern of the normal acquisition of gender identity from which they were seen to deviate. It was a response to the inability of existing discourses to account effectively for hysterical and other psychosomatic symptoms, produced mainly by middle-class women patients in late nineteenth-century Vienna. Through analyses of patients which used linguistic techniques of free association, hypnosis and the analysis of dreams, fantasies and parapraxes (jokes, slips of the tongue, temporary forgetfulness), Freud developed a theory of gender acquisition which made gendered subjectivity the key to identity. It accounted for psychic disturbance in later life in terms of problems in the early acquisition of feminine or masculine subjectivity, locating its origin in the psychic structures of sexual identity acquired in the early years of childhood.

In opposition to existing views of gender, childhood and sexuality, which saw gender identity as inborn and sexuality as an effect of puberty, Freud asserted that individuals were sexual beings from birth. Moreover, he claimed that infants were initially neither feminine nor masculine but 'polymorphously perverse' and capable of developing either normal feminine or masculine identities or neither. The paths whereby girls developed normal feminine psyches and boys masculine identities involved, according to Freud, complex psycho-sexual processes which were completed in the first five years of life and which were critical for the psychic constitution of the future adult. The acquisition of psychic femininity or masculinity by the biological female or male involved the repression of those features of the child's initial bisexuality which were incompatible with the sexual identity in question. The acquisition of sexual identity involved the formation in the individual of the unconscious as the site of socially taboo desires which, psychoanalysis claims, constantly seek to disrupt conscious life and are responsible for the meaning of dreams and parapraxes as well as for psychic disorders.

It is the stress in Freudian theory on the initial bisexuality of the child and the precarious psychic rather than biological nature of gender identity which has encouraged many feminists to attempt to appropriate psychoanalysis for their interests. At one level Freudian theory marks a radical break with biological determinism by making the structures of psychic development the foundations of *social* organization. This occurs in the context of the nuclear family and, in normal development, leads to the acquisition by children of a heterosexual gendered identity. Yet the degree to which structures of psycho-sexual development, which have a universal status in Freudian theory, can be seen as fully social is open to question, since they are neither historically nor culturally specific. It would be more accurate to ascribe to them a status similar in kind to that of biological sex as the universal preconditions for social organization. None the less the insistence on the psycho-sexual rather than biological structuring of gender identity and on gender acquisition as a precarious process, constantly threatened by the return of the repressed, means that gender identity is not fixed by psycho-analysis in the same way or to the same degree, as it is in biological determinism. Gender identity is contained within fixed psycho-sexual structures which are the precondition for all subjectivity and which allow for the abnormal as well as the normal. However, in its claims to provide a universal theory, psychoanalysis reduces gender to an effect of pre-given, psycho-sexual processes and closes off questions of gender identity from history.

Feminists who use psychoanalytic theory in their analyses argue that in accepting the Freudian model, they are not endorsing patriarchal forms of heterosexuality and the nuclear family but the precariousness of sexual identity which underlies those structures and which could easily take another non-repressive form. Yet, while for Freud sexual normativity is precarious, heterosexuality is none the less the norm. The alternative to heterosexuality and the patriarchal nuclear family is either illness or homosexuality which is by definition the result of immature psycho-sexual development. In order to avoid this problem, feminist Freudians have sought to restrict the Freudian model to the patriarchal structures of capitalist society and the nuclear family. Yet whether the Freudian model of psycho-sexual development is seen to explain the acquisition of gender identity universally or under patriarchal capitalism, it does rely on processes which attribute meaning to visible anatomical sexual difference. Freud was both explicit and emphatic about the role of anatomical sexual difference in the acquisition of psychic gender, an anatomical difference which focused on the presence or absence of the penis.

The process of the acquisition of gendered subjectivity in Freud involves the structuring of innate drives, which are initially neither feminine nor masculine. The mechanisms through which an infant acquires a conscious and unconscious gender identity are the castration and Oedipus complexes. These processes are resolved in different ways in the case of girls and boys, and Freud's account of them is clearest in the case of masculinity, which is taken as the norm against which difference is measured. Freud assumes that young boys recognize the absence of the penis, the organ of male sexual gratification, in girls and women, and that this provokes in them a fear of castration. This encourages them not to compete with the father figure in the family for sexual possession of the mother, but to identify with the position of the father, and to postpone sexual gratification to the future.

For young girls, the acquisition of femininity involves a recognition that they are already castrated like their mother. This recognition is said to provoke a disgusted turning away from the mother as initial love object, the transference of desire to the father and the promise of satisfaction at some future point through bearing a male child. Women can never directly exercise the power invested in the position of father because they do not have a penis, and this biological fact has, in Freud, important psychic consequences for feminine subjectivity. This is made most clear in Freud's controversial essay on 'Some psychical consequences of the anatomical distinction between the sexes' (Freud, 1977). In this essay, Freud describes how recognition of the girl's lack of a penis provokes a different response in girls and boys, but in both cases, a response which assumes the desirability of the organ. Boys will either feel 'horror at the mutilated creature or triumphant contempt for her' and these reactions will determine their future attitude to women (Freud, 1977, p. 336). 'A little girl', Freud continues, 'behaves differently. She makes her judgement and her decision in a flash. She has seen it and knows that she is without it and wants to have it' (Freud, 1977, p. 336). Penis envy may result either in a masculinity complex in which the girl hopes she will one day get a penis or pretends that she has one and behaves as if she were a man, or in a recognition of inferiority and contempt for herself and the female sex in general. This response results in the specific character traits of jealousy, the rejection of masturbation, the equation of the penis with a child and the desire to have a child by her father. This amounts to a culturally – and historically – specific discourse about what constitutes 'normal' heterosexual femininity.

The different ways in which the Oedipus complex is resolved for girls and boys is also crucial in determining the qualities of normal femininity and masculinity:

> In boys . . . the complex is not simply repressed, it is literally smashed to pieces by the shock of threatened castration. Its libidinal cathexes are abandoned, desexualised and in part sublimated; its objects are incorporated into the ego where they form the nucleus of the superego and give that new structure its characteristic qualities . . .

> In girls the motive for the demolition of the Oedipus complex is lacking. Castration has already had its effect, which was to force the child into the situation of the Oedipus complex. Thus the Oedipus complex escapes the

fate which it meets with in boys; it may be slowly abandoned or dealt with by repression or its effects may persist far into women's normal mental life. I cannot evade the notion (though I hestitate to give it expression) that for women the level of what is ethically normal is different from what it is for men. Character traits which critics of every epoch have brought up against women – that they show less sense of justice than men, that they are less ready to submit to the great exigencies of life, that they are more often influenced in their judgements by feelings of affection or hostility – all these would be amply accounted for by the modification in the formation of their superego which we have inferred above. We must not allow ourselves to be deflected from such conclusions by the denials of the feminists, who are anxious to force us to regard the two sexes as completely equal in position and worth; but we shall, of course, willingly agree that the majority of men are also far behind the masculine ideal and that all human individuals, as a result of their bisexual disposition and of cross-inheritance, combine in themselves both masculine and feminine characteristics, so that pure masculinity and pure femininity remain theoretical constructions of un-certain content. (Freud, 1977, p. 341–2)

It may seem as if Freudian terms accurately describe the negative sides of femininity in a society in which it is repressed. The primacy of the penis as principal signifier of sexual difference could be read in symbolic terms, as a signifier of power in a society in which men are dominant and control social institutions, including the family. Yet even here problems remain. The attempt to avoid the inevitable patriarchal con-sequences of psycho-sexual development by making it the historical product of a culture which is patriarchal, but need not always be, is fraught with difficulties. Freudian theory uses visible anatomical difference as its guarantee of psychic difference and women's inferiority. Yet it does not explain why social relations should take this form. It assumes that they are a manifestation of the nature of *man*. This gives rise to the problem of how anatomical difference can ever acquire a different status and meaning in which femininity is either of equal value or cultural norms of femininity and masculinity are dissolved. Furthermore, feminists might wish to question both psychoanalytic assumptions about feminine and masculine qualities and the psychoanalytic practice of reducing these qualities and subjective identity to sexual difference, whether this is psychic, biological or socially constructed.

In Freud, the femininity or masculinity which the normal adult must achieve through her or his psycho-sexual development represent culturally and historically specific forms of gender identity. These assume a universal status. The social structures which guarantee psycho-sexual development are also fixed and involve an acceptance of the universality of the Oedipal triangle and the incest taboo. These social norms underpinning psycho-analytic theory receive their clearest expression in the structural anthropology of Lévi-Strauss, who, in an attempt to develop a universal theory of human society, makes the incest taboo and the exchange of women by men the founding principles of all cultures. For feminists, the key questions must be whether this ahistoricism is politically and theoretically useful, and whether it is possible or desirable to develop a psychoanalytic model which does not make universal claims but is historically and socially specific.

A feminist poststructuralist perspective on these questions suggests that we cannot begin with a general theory of the psyche. If we assume that subjectivity is discursively produced in social institutions and processes, there is no pre-given reason why we should privilege sexual relations above other forms of social relations as constitutive of identity. There may, of course, be historically specific reasons for doing this in a particular analysis, but they will not be universal. Furthermore, if we are concerned specifically with the question of sexual identity, then psychoanalysis itself must be looked at as one discourse among many which has been influential in constituting inherently patriarchal norms of sexuality. Feminist poststructuralism suggests that it is not good enough to assume that psychoanalysis accurately describes the structures of femininity and masculinity under patriarchy, since discourse constitutes rather than reflects meaning. To take psychoanalysis as descriptive is to assume basic patriarchal structures which exist prior to their discursive realization.

Lacan's Appropriation of Freud

Attempts to move away from the centrality of anatomical difference in the acquisition of psychic sexual identity in Freud have prompted some feminists to turn their attention to the works of Jacques Lacan.[2] Aspects of Lacan's development of Freudian psychoanalysis have influenced the model of ideology and subjectivity found in Althusserian Marxism and much feminist thinking about language, sexuality and subjectivity. In his reading of Freud, Lacan stresses the linguistic structure of the unconscious as a site of repressed meanings and the *imaginary* structure of subjectivity acquired, like the unconscious, at the point of entry of the individual as speaking subject into the *symbolic* order of language, laws, social processes and institutions.

The imaginary is a term used to describe the pre-Oedipal identification of the infant with its mirror image, an identification guaranteed by the gaze of the mother holding the child to the mirror. At this stage in its development, the child is neither feminine nor masculine, and has yet to acquire language. The mirror phase begins a process in which the child will eventually acquire gendered subjectivity and a place in the symbolic order. This process involves the resolution of the Oedipal and castration complexes. It creates in the individual a structure of subjectivity which ensures that the individual, as speaking subject, will be caught in a misrecognition of itself as the *Other*. The Other is the position of control of desire, power and meaning. Desire is a product of language and is subject to the constant deferral of satisfaction equivalent to the constant deferral of meaning in language. To control the one would be to control the other. In identifying with the position of the Other, the subject misrecognizes itself as the source of meaning and the power that structures it and of which it is an effect. The symbolic order in Lacanian theory is the social and cultural order in which we live our lives as conscious, gendered subjects. It is structured by language and the laws and social institutions which language guarantees.

Each time an individual assumes a subject position within language, the mechanisms of the mirror phase and of psychosexual development are involved. They guarantee that the individual's identification with the position of speaking subject is imaginary and is invested with the massive psychic energy of the desire to control meaning. The mirror phase is, for Lacan, the child's first intelligent act and involves identification with the image of its physical form, reflected in a mirror. Through watching itself gesture, the child is able to experience 'in play the relation between the movements assumed in the image and the reflected environment, and between this virtual complex and the reality it reduplicates – the child's own body, and the persons and things around him' (Lacan, 1977, p. 1). In other words, the child's ego becomes split into the I which is watching and the I which is watched. Because of this split, the unity and imagined control which the child's identification with its mirror image brings is imaginary. A second splitting of the ego occurs with entry into the symbolic order after the resolution of the castration and Oedipus complexes. The resolution of these complexes brings about the gender specific organization of the drives, the psyche and the unconscious. The secondary split is between the I which speaks and the I which is represented in the utterance. Just as the infant of the mirror phase misrecognizes itself as unified and in physical control of itself, so the speaking subject in the symbolic order misrecognizes itself and its utterance as one and assumes that it is the author of meaning.

As in Saussurean theory, the symbolic order is made up of signifiers, but with an important difference. Signifiers are not linked to fixed signifieds or concepts. Language is a constant stream of signifiers which achieve temporary meaning for a speaking subject retrospectively through their difference from one another. Lacan's theory of language has much in common with Jacques Derrida's radical critique of rationalist theories of language, consciousness and the *logocentric* tradition of Western metaphysics, which presuppose that the meaning of concepts is fixed prior to their articulation in language.[3] Derrida extended and transformed Saussure's principle that meaning is produced by the difference between signs in the language chain. He questioned even an arbitrary fixed identity between signifier and signified. As for Derrida, meaning for Lacan can only occur in a specific textual location and in a relation of difference from all other textual locations. In Lacanian psychoanalysis it is the mechanisms of desire, rather the principle of *différance*, that prevents the final fixing of meaning.

In Lacanian theory, however, signification is not a process of infinite free play, as it is for Derrida, in which all meaning is temporary and relative. For Lacan, meaning and the symbolic order as a whole, is fixed in relation to a primary, transcendental signifier which Lacan calls the *phallus*, the signifier of sexual difference, which guarantees the patriarchal structure of the symbolic order. The phallus signifies power and control in the symbolic order through control of the satisfaction of desire, the primary source of power within psychoanalytic theory.

Lacanian theory assumes desire to be the motivating principle of human life. It is a concept drawn from the Freudian account of psycho-sexual development in which the infant is unable to control the satisfaction of its own needs and demands. This lack of control is symbolized by the periodic withdrawal of the mother's breast. The desire for control through possession becomes the primary motivating force of the psyche and control is identified with the position of the father and symbolically represented by the phallus.

In reality no one can control desire since no one can occupy the position of the Other, the structuring principle of human culture, and become the source of language rather than an effect of it. The lack of control which the individual experiences as the gap between need, demand and satisfaction is, as in Freud, the motive for language, which is a never-ending attempt to control it by becoming the origin and the guarantee of meaning. The status of the phallus and the position of the father as 'Other' in Lacanian theory is primarily symbolic. No individual man can actually occupy the position of the 'Other', the position, for example, of God the Father in the Judaic-Christian tradition, who is the source of the law and controls meaning and access to the satisfaction of desire.

Yet even though control of desire is impossible, anatomical sexual difference does have a role to play in who can aspire to the phallus. As Jacqueline Rose argues in *Feminine Sexuality. Jacques Lacan and the Ecole Freudienne*:

> Sexual difference is then assigned according to whether individual subjects do or do not possess the phallus, which means not that anatomical difference *is* sexual difference (the one as strictly deducible from the other), but that anatomical difference come to *figure* sexual difference, that is, it becomes the sole representative of what that difference is allowed to be. It thus covers over the complexity of the child's early sexual life with a crude opposition in which that very complexity is refused or repressed. The phallus thus indicates the reduction of difference to an instance of visible perception a *seeming* value. (Mitchell and Rose, 1982, p. 42)

The fact that values are illusory or that men, like women, are produced by and subject to the symbolic order and never in control does not detract from the social implications of these illusions. As in Freudian theory, male anatomy has a crucial role to play in determining female and male access to the symbolic order. Despite Lacan's own protestations to the contrary, Lacanian theory employs an anatomically grounded elision between the phallus and the penis which implies the necessary patriarchal organization of desire and sexuality. This organization is as fixed as the Oedipal structure itself. Men, by virtue of their penis, can aspire to a position of power and control within the symbolic order. Women, on the other hand, have no position in the symbolic order, except in relation to men, as mothers, and even the process of mothering is given patriarchal meanings, reduced, in Freud, to an effect of penis envy. The theory that women have no access to the symbolic order in their own right has led feminists to develop theories of women's language as a constant, repressed threat to the patriarchal symbolic order. These theories are discussed later in this chapter.

Feminist Appropriations of Psychoanalysis

From the time when Freud's work first began to be influential women psychoanalysts have attempted to rewrite aspects of Freudian theory in ways which make it more acceptable to women. This rewriting has concentrated on giving new meanings to psycho-sexual development, usually by an explicit appeal to actual historical social norms and values, or on developing new theories of female sexuality and subjectivity. In both cases attention has shifted from the castration complex and the resolution of the Oedipus complex to the pre-Oedipal relationship with the mother.[4]

As early as 1917, Karen Horney argued that Freud's assumption of the parallel psycho-sexual development of girls and boys, which is distinguished by their different reaction to the absence or presence of the penis, might be 'the expression of a one-sidedness in our observations, due to their being made from the man's point of view' (Baker Miller, 1973, p. 9). Staying within the framework of Freudian analysis, she suggested that it is possible to substitute for the importance of the penis the 'by no means negligible physiological superiority of the female capacity for motherhood' (p. 10). This would motivate male 'envy of pregnancy, childbirth and motherhood as well as of the breasts and of the act of suckling', which Horney claimed to have discovered in her psychoanalysis of men (p. 10). This alternative reading of the meanings produced by patients well illustrates the degree to which psychoanalytic practice depends on the assumptions of the analyst for its results. Writing of her own 'discovery' of the female child's fear of vaginal injury in penetration, Horney commented 'Since the possibility of such a connection occurred to me, I have learned to construe in this sense – i.e. as representing the dread of vaginal injury – many phenomena that I was previously content to interpret as castrating fantasies in the male sense' (p. 15, fn.). Horney's rewriting of the meaning of psycho-sexual development appeals to the social values of the society in which she lived. It involves making signifiers such as the penis and the breast, which in Freud have universal fixed meanings, relative and plural. She concludes, for example, that the theory of female penis envy could itself be construed as the result of male envy, just as male creativity in science and the arts might be seen as over-compensation for men's lack of procreative power.

More recent feminist attempts to rewrite the process of female psycho-sexual development have also concentrated on giving new meanings to the features of femininity proposed by Freud. The tendency in the very different work of Nancy Chodorow, Luce Irigaray and Hélène Cixous, for example, has been to concentrate on the importance of the pre-Oedipal phase of psycho-sexual development – that time before femininity or masculinity when the infant is in a symbiotic relationship with her mother. For Chodorow, this phase is the starting point for a new social theory of gender acquisition; for Irigaray and Cixous, it is the point at which femininity has not yet been repressed by patriarchy and women have not yet become man-made. Luce Irigaray goes beyond Freud and Lacan to produce a radical theory of the feminine libido, based on female sexuality and auto-eroticism which celebrates the female body in separation from men. Her work, together with that of Julia Kristeva and Hélène Cixous, will be discussed in detail later in the chapter.

Both Freudian and Lacanian psychoanalysis propose universal structures and processes within which individuals acquire precarious 'normal' heterosexual femininity or masculinity, or deviate abnormally from them. While normal gender identity is constantly threatened by the return of the repressed, it is none the less fixed by psycho-sexual structures, and social relations are read in terms of these fixed structures. In the work of Lacan, the structures produce subject positions within the symbolic order which are determined by their relation to the phallus as signifier of sexual difference. The tendency of feminist psycho-analytic theory which, like Freudian and Lacanian theory, assumes a fixed set of structures within which femininity is acquired, is also to theorize femininity in separation from the social, and to prioritize the psycho-sexual over the historically social. This can be seen, for example, in the work of Juliet Mitchell. In her influential text, *Psychoanalysis and Feminism* (1975), which did much to restore feminist interest in psychoanalysis after Kate Millett's onslaught, Mitchell argues that Freudian and Lacanian psychoanalysis provide a useful conceptual framework for understanding the construction of human sexuality. She suggests that the apparent phallocentrism of psychoanalysis is descriptive of the state of society rather than a precondition of human sociality. Mitchell avoids confronting the anatomical determinism in psychoanalysis, which leads women to be defined in terms of lack. Instead, *Psychoanalysis and Femininism* concentrates on the *symbolic* status of the phallus, the Law of the Father and subject positions within the symbolic order. Although the phallus is the signifier of sexual difference, Mitchell argues that it is not necessarily tied to particular patriarchal social relations. Writing in *Women: the Longest Revolution*, she reiterates this point:

> Whatever their anatomical sex, all babies will form their sexual identifications with whatever is signified on each side to the line that is drawn by the presence or absence of the phallus. What is signified is, however, not fixed in advance . . .
>
> Thus, for instance, the penis and he who possesses it (the father) come to be signified by, but they are not identical with, the phallus which as a signifying term can move around giving us such important concepts and observations as the unconscious phallic mother. (Mitchell, 1984, p. 245)

In Mitchell's appropriation of psychoanalysis the plurality of the phallus as signifying term is limited to the realm of individual, psycho-sexual organization. Attempts to situate psychoanalytic theory of the psychic construction of gender within an historically specific social environment which allows for the possibility of change, for example, the work of Nancy Chodorow, inevitably require a transformation of key Freudian categories and the anthropological assumptions upon which they are based. What in Freud and Lacan are abstract positions with which the child identifies, for example, the position of father, become real people in Chodorow's work. Working in the American context, Nancy Chodorow is anxious to use psycho-analysis to answer biological and social theories of gender acquisition which deny the importance of unconscious mental processes. Instead of privileging the Oedipus and castration complexes, she focuses on the psychic effects of the pre-Oedipal phase of development and on the quality of the mother–daughter relationship, as compared to mother–son and father–son relation-ships. Nancy Chodorow's theory is outlined in a short chapter in *Women, Culture and Society* (Rosaldo and Lamphere, 1974) and developed in detail in *The Reproduction of Mothering* (1978). Accepting pre-Oedipal bisexuality, Chodorow stresses the importance of 'the fact that women universally are largely responsible for early childcare and for (at least) later female socialization' . . . 'This points to the central importance of the mother–daughter relationship for women, and to a focus on the conscious and unconscious effects of early involvement with a female for children of both sexes. The fact that males and females experience this social environment differently as they grow up accounts for the development of basic sex differences in personality' (Rosaldo and Lamphere, 1974, p. 44).

Chodorow argues that mothering involves a woman in a double identification, with her mother and with her child, in which she repeats her own mother–child history. This results in a stronger bond between mother and daughter than between mother and son and a lesser degree of individuation in the case of girls, who consequently develop more flexible ego boundaries which create the psychological preconditions for the reproduction of women's subordination to men. In contrast, mothers en-courage their sons to differentiate themselves from their mother and develop a masculine identity based on their father or father substitute:

> However a boy's father is relatively more remote than his mother. He rarely plays a major caretaking role even at this

period in his son's life [the pre-Oedipal stage]. In most societies, his work and social life take place farther from the home than do those of his wife. He is, then, often relatively inaccessible to his son and performs his male role activities away from where the son spends most of his life. As a result, a boy's male gender identification often becomes a 'positional' identification, with aspects of his father's clearly or not-so-clearly defined male role, rather than a more generalized 'personal' identification – a diffuse identification with his father's personality, values and behavioural traits – that could grow out of a real relationship to his father. (Rosaldo and Lamphere, 1974, p. 49)

The difference that Chodorow posits between 'real' personal and positional identification is the definitive factor in her account of the differential constitution of femininity and masculinity. Moreover, the problematic process of differentiation from the mother is said to account for the boy's 'repression and devaluation of femininity on both the psychological and cultural levels' (p. 51).

The effects of the different types of male and female pre-Oedipal relationship, together with the differential resolution of the Oedipus complex in girls and boys, which are dealt with in detail in *The Reproduction of Mothering*, have the effect of making women open to a range of 'equally deep and primary relationships, especially with their children, and, more importantly, with other women' (Rosaldo and Lamphere, 1974, p. 53). Men lack the extended personal relations which women have and 'their relationships with other men tend to be based not on particularistic connection or affective ties, but rather on abstract, universalistic role expectations' (p. 53). These masculine traits are seen both as negative for the individual concerned and as prerequisites for the reproduction of patriarchy.

Given its effects on the acquisition of gender, women's primary responsibility for parenting has important social implications:

Women's mothering, then, produces psychological self-definition and capacities appropriate to mothering in women, and curtails and inhibits these capacities and this self-definition in men. The early experience of being cared for by a woman produces a fundamental structure of expectations in women and men concerning mothers' lack of separate interests from their infants and total concern for their infants' welfare. Daughters grow up identifying with these mothers, about whom they have such expectations. This set of expectations is generalized to the assumption that women naturally take care of children of all ages and the belief that women's 'maternal' qualities can and should be extended to the nonmothering work that they do. All these results of women's mothering have ensured that women will mother infants and will take continuing responsibility for children.

The reproduction of mothering is the basis for the reproduction of women's location and responsibilities in the domestic sphere. This mothering, and its generalization to women's structural location in the domestic sphere, links the contemporary social organization of gender and social organization of production and contributes to the reproduction of each. That women mother is a fundamental organizational feature of the sex–gender system. It is basic to the sexual division of labour and generates a psychology and ideology of male dominance as well as an ideology about women's capacities and nature. Women, as wives and mothers, contribute as well to the daily and generational reproduction, both physical and psychological, of male workers and thus to the reproduction of capitalist production.

Women's mothering also reproduces the family as it is constituted in male-dominated society. The sexual and familial division of labor in which women mother creates a sexual division of psychic organization and orientation. It produces socially gendered women and men who enter into asymmetrical heterosexual relationships; it produces men who react to, fear, and act superior to women, and who put most of their energies into the nonfamilial work world and do not parent. Finally it produces women who turn their energies towards nurturing and caring for children – in turn reproducing the sexual and familial division of labour in which women mother. (Chodorow, 1978, pp. 208–9)

Chodorow's theorization of the psychic structures of femininity and masculinity in terms of the practice of parenting, rather than the abstract and universal positionality of the Oedipus complex opens up the possibility, at least in theory, of changing gender norms through the transformation of the social organization of family life. The greater personal involvement of men in childcare would, Chodorow argues, radically transform the quality of the psycho-sexual structures of masculinity and femininity and create the preconditions for the abolition of the sexual division of labour. It is a process which requires political action:

We live in a period when the demands of the roles defined by the sex–gender system have created widespread discomfort and resistance. Aspects of this sytem are in crisis internally and conflict with economic tendencies. Change will certainly occur, but the outcome is far from certain. The elimination of the present organization of parenting in favour of a system in which both men and women are responsible would be a tremendous social advance. This outcome is historically possible, but far from inevitable. Such advances do not occur simply because they are better for 'society', and certainly not simply because they are better for some (usually less powerful) people. They depend on the conscious organization and activity of all women and men who recognise that their interests lie in transforming the social organization of gender and eliminating sex inequality. (p. 219)

Although changes in primary parenting may well be fundamental to the transformation of patriarchy, this programme for change appears over-optimistic because it is necessarily reductionist. Chodorow herself stresses that she is concerned with the reproduction of mothering, not with gender as a whole. Yet the privileging of mothering in the acquisition of gendered subjectivity means that all the other processes through which subjectivity is constituted are necessarily subject to this primary structuring and the gender inequality to which it gives rise. Moreover, changes in the gendered subjectivity of the already constituted individual can only come about through psychoanalysis.

While moves to locate the acquisition of unconscious structures of subjectivity within an historical and cultural context are to be welcomed, from a poststructuralist perspective this type of appropriation of Freudian psychoanalysis has several important disadvantages. It continues to privilege universal structures of psycho-sexual development, with a new emphasis on pre-Oedipal relationships. This leads to a reading of existing social relations which are patriarchal, and class- and race-specific, in terms of pre-given psychic structures. It reproduces the politically significant restriction, within psychoanalysis, of subjectivity to sexual identity, and the constitution of this identity to the first five years of childhood. At the same time it loses sight of Freud's radical deconstruction of the ego, replacing it with a stable gendered subjectivity, founded on gender roles learnt in the context of the unconscious psychic structuring of femininity and masculinity which reinforces them.

As with all psychoanalysis, the central problem lies in the attempt to theorize structures of femininity and masculinity on the basic of fixed psycho-sexual structures which look to a single cause. In Freud it is the Oedipus and castration complexes, in Chodorow, pre-Oedipal relations. However, Chodorow's attempt to make pre-Oedipal relations social rather than ahistorically psycho-sexual creates a productive tension. On the one hand Chodorow acknowledges that women's social role as mother is always historically and culturally specific in its organization, social meanings and value. On the other, she sees mothering and its psycho-sexual and social implications as common to all societies. This tension produces a position where what has always been is not inevitable. Yet to progress further on this front we need to deconstruct the centrality of sexuality itself.

Rewriting Female Sexuality:
French Feminist Psychoanalysis

In the work of the French psychoanalyst, Luce Irigaray, femininity is theorized as an effect of the organization of female desire in a female libido. Female libido is not constituted by a lack, as in Freud, but by female sexuality which is fundamentally other to male sexuality. Extending the Lacanian concept of the phallocentric patriarchal order. Irigaray argues that the otherness of female sexuality has been repressed by patriarchy, which seeks to theorize it within masculine parameters. This is the main argument of Irigaray's influential text *This sex which is not one* (1985), extracts of which are available in Marks and de Courtrivron (1981). Irigaray argues that the patriarchal definition of female sexuality caused women to lose touch with their essential femininity which is located in the female body and its capacity for multiple and heterogeneous pleasure. As in Lacanian psychoanalysis, the acquisition of language produces desire and women's language is motivated by the attempts to satisfy desire. However, just as women's libido is other to men's, so women's language is necessarily distinct from male language. The bisexuality of Freudian psychoanalysis is superseded in Irigaray's work by distinct female and male libidos. It offers a theory of the 'female' rather than the 'feminine', however this distinction is less clear in French where the adjective *féminin* encompasses both the English adjectives 'female' and 'feminine'.

Irigaray argues for an integral relationship between sexuality and language. In her view, female sexual pleasure is fundamentally autoerotic and plural. While male sexuality is concentrated on the penis, women have a multiplicity of sexual organs:

But a woman touches herself by and within herself directly, without mediation, and before any distinction between activity and passivity is possible. A woman 'touches herself' constantly without anyone being able to forbid her to do so, for her sex is composed of two lips which embrace continually . . . Her sexuality always at least double is in fact plural . . . Indeed women's pleasure does not have to choose between clitoral activity and vaginal passivity, for example. The pleasure of the vaginal caress does not have to substitute itself for the pleasure of the clitoral caress [as in the Freudian version]. Both contribute irreplaceably to women's pleasure but they are only two caresses among many to do so. (Marks and de Courtivron, 1981, p. 102)

Female desire is seen as totally foreign to male desire and the two can only be brought together through a patriarchal repression of the female. The otherness of female desire is the basis of the otherness of female language. Just as a 'woman has sex organs just about everywhere' (p. 103), so her language is non-linear and incoherent, and incomprehensible to male language, with its focus on the logic of reason:

In her statements – at least when she dares to speak out – woman retouches herself constantly. She just barely separates from herself some chatter, an exclamation, a half-secret, a sentence left in suspense – When she returns to it, it is only to set out again from another point of pleasure or pain. One must listen to her differently in order to hear an 'other meaning' which is constantly in the process of weaving itself, at the same time ceaselessly embracing words and yet casting them off to avoid becoming fixed, immobilized. For when she 'says' something, it is already no longer identical to what she means. Moreover her statements are never identical to anything. Their distinguishing feature is one of contiguity. They touch (upon). And when they wander too far from this nearness, she stops and begins again from 'zero': her body–sex organ. (p. 103)

The implications of this theory are clear. In orthodox

psychoanalysis femininity is a psychic construct organized in relation to sexual difference, but based on an initial bisexuality. For Irigaray, the psychic is never bisexual but always male or female. When freed from their patriarchal definition and the repression of their sexuality, women are assumed to be fundamentally different from men and their use of language is other than the logical language of the symbolic order. Male sexuality and desire, in the form of the phallus, is the organizing principle of the symbolic order and the source of the type of rational language through which social power is exercised. There is no space for resistance within the terms of the symbolic order, and women who do not wish to repress their true femaleness can have no access to it. Both women and men are exclusively defined in terms of their sexuality but for women this involves an abdication of any claim to the symbolic order and a retreat into homoeroticism and femaleness as separateness.

While many women may wish to see the emergence of a female sexuality which is not constructed by and in the interests of men, to make such a sexuality the basis for women's language is politically dangerous, since it reduces women to a version of their sexuality. This theory marks one possible conclusion to the psychoanalytic assumption that language is motivated by sexual desire and that subjectivity, acquired in language, is no more than an effect of sexual identity. Irigaray is much more explicit about the link between biology and identity than Lacan. The shift of emphasis from the positionality of the Oedipus complex, organized around the phallus, the signifier of male desire, to female sexual pleasure offers women a positive interpretation of their bodies. They are no longer defined in terms of lack. It is, however, the meanings given to the female body and to female desire which are particularly worrying for a feminism anxious to transform existing social relations rather than to live alongside them in separation from them in a social order that remains patriarchal.

The connection which Lacanian psychoanalysis makes between feminine and masculine libido (the gender-specific organization of the drives on the basis of repression), the unconscious and language, is also central to the work of Hélène Cixous which focuses on the relationship between feminine libido and feminine writing. Her work stresses feminine heterogeneity. Like Irigaray, Cixous sees feminine sexuality as rich and plural and she draws a parallel between feminine libido and writing. She looks to feminine writing for challenge to the patriarchal order.

Whereas Luce Irigaray links feminine libido with biological femaleness, Cixous is ambivalent about fixing it biologically. Her work is influenced by the anti-essentialism of Derrida's deconstruction and she brings together his notion of logocentrism and phallocentrism. She argues that masculine sexuality and masculine language are phallocentric and logocentric, seeking to fix meaning through a set of binary oppositions, for example, father/mother, head/heart, intelligible/sensitive, logos/pathos, which rely for their meaning on a primary binary opposition of male/female (or penis/lack of penis) which guarantees and reproduces the patriarchal order. This hierarchization of meaning serves to subordinate the feminine to the masculine order.

Feminine libido and feminine language, which are repressed by patriarchy, exceed and threaten its phallocentrism and logocentrism. Feminine libido has its source in the pre-Oedipal phase, the time before repression, femininity and masculinity, when the infant is in an all-encompassing imaginary relationship with its mother. In the post-Oedipal phase, the feminine is most often located in the unconscious, repressed by the structures of phallocentrism. The patriarchal society which this repression supports accepts male libido, male definitions of female libido and male writing as the norm for both women and men (Marks and de Courtivron, 1981, p. 249). Yet, Cixous argues, the phallocentric, logocentric order is not unassailable, feminine writing can challenge it:

> The challenging of this solidarity of logocentrism and phallocentrism has today become insistent enough – the bringing to light of the fate which has been imposed upon woman, of her burial – to threaten the stability of the masculine edifice which passed itself off as eternal–natural; by bringing forth from the world of femininity reflections, hypotheses which are necessarily ruinous for the bastion

which still holds the authority. What would become of logocentrism, of the great philosophical systems, of world order in general if the rock upon which they founded their church were to crumble? If it were to come out in a new day that the logocentric project had always been, undeniably, to *found* (fund) phallocentrism, to insure for masculine order a rationale equal to history itself? Then all the stories would have to be told differently, the future would be incalculable, the historical forces would, will, change hands, bodies; another thinking as yet not thinkable will transform the functioning of all society. Well we are living through this very period when the conceptual foundation of a millenial culture is in process of being undermined by millions of a species of mole as not yet recognised. (Marks and de Courtivron, 1981, pp. 92–3)

This emphasis on writing, as opposed to speech, is a mark of the influence of deconstruction on Cixous's work. It avoids the metaphysics of presence in which the speaking subject is the guarantee of meaning, and in this way avoids tying feminine and masculine language to the biological sex of the speaking subject. Yet the very otherness of feminine writing means that it cannot be prescribed in advance:

It is impossible to *define* a feminine practice of writing, and this is an impossibility that will remain, for this practice can never be theorized, enclosed, coded – which doesn't mean that it doesn't exist. But it will always surpass the discourse that regulates the phallocentric system; it does and will take place in areas other than those subordinated to philosophico-theoretical domination. It will be conceived of only by subjects who are breakers of automatisms, by peripheral figures that no authority can ever subjugate. (p. 253)

None the less, in an explicitly feminist move which limits the free play of language, Cixous links feminine writing under patriarchy with women. Women are the likely subjects of feminine libido. Cixous gives two reasons why this should be the case. On the one hand, in a move into essentialism, similar to Irigaray's, she links feminine libido with the female sexual organs. On the other hand, Cixous gestures towards an historical perspective in which both feminine and masculine libidos are constructed in particular but not necessarily universal ways under patriarchy. The concern with real power relations implicit in this move aligns Cixous more closely with feminism as a political movement. Writing becomes a way of giving voice to repressed female sexuality and the female libido which it sustains:

> By writing her self, woman will return to the body which has been more than confiscated from her, which has been turned into the uncanny stranger on display – the ailing or dead figure, which so often turns out to be the nasty companion, the cause and location of inhibitions. Censor the body and you censor breath and speech at the same time.

> Write your self. Your body must be heard. Only then will the immense resources of the unconscious spring forth. Our naphtha will spread, throughout the world, without dollars – black or gold – nonassessed values that will change the rules of the old game. (p. 250)

Cixous's appropriation of Lacanian psychoanalysis is relatively optimistic about the possibility of transforming the patriarchal symbolic order through giving women a new sense of themselves, repressed until now, and asserting different feminine meanings and values at present repressed by patriarchy. In the struggle to reassert feminine values, feminine writing, which draws on the unconscious, is a key site for bringing about change.

Writing is also the focus of attention in the work of Julia Kristeva. She uses the Lacanian concepts of the symbolic order and the subject to form the basis of a theory of signifying practice, *signifiance*, which emphasizes the disruptive and potentially revolutionary force for subjectivity of the marginal and repressed aspects of language. Kristeva accepts Lacan's theory of the phallocentric symbolic order and concludes that 'woman', in the sense of the feminine, has no access to language. The patriarchal symbolic order represses 'woman', whose meanings lie beyond 'language and sociality' (Marks and de Courtivron, 1981, p. 138). Kristeva's use of the signifier 'woman' is deconstructive in the sense that she argues that there is no essential womanhood, not even a repressed one and that feminist practice cannot be directed at achieving or recovering some sort of essential state. It can only be defined in terms of what it rejects and what it is not. Politically the notion of being a woman is at best a useful, temporary political strategy for organizing campaigns on behalf of women's interests as they are currently defined within patriarchy (p. 137).

Kristeva's emphasis on feminine and masculine modes of language rather than on women and men is integral to her theory of subjectivity. It marks a shift from biological sexual difference to subjectivity as purely an effect of language which has feminine and masculine aspects. Language, however, is central to the power relations of the social order. Kristeva argues that the structure of the symbolic order posits a transcendent, self-present subject, the equivalent of Lacan's 'Other', who is the source of symbolic meaning. This subject is fixed in a subject–object relation which underpins the syntactical structure of language in which what Kristeva calls *thetic* subjectivity is constituted. The misrecognized position of the transcendental subject is an effect of phallocentric and logocentric discourse which represses the feminine to achieve these effects.

However, like Cixous, Kristeva argues that there are feminine forms of signification which cannot be contained by the rational, thetic structure of the symbolic order and which therefore threaten its sovereignty and have been relegated to the margins of discourse. Yet unlike Cixous, Kristeva does not locate feminine aspects of language in women's female libido. The feminine is a mode of language, open to male and female writers. As she argues in *Revolution in Poetic Language* (1984), the return of the repressed feminine is manifest, for example, in the 'marginal' discourse of the literary avant-garde, such as the poetry of Lautréamont and Mallarmé and the prose of James

Joyce. These texts are seen as exceeding phallocentric, logocentric discourse, putting the subjectivity which supports it into question and showing subjectivity *in process.*

Feminine modes of signification are other to the language of the symbolic order and are termed *semiotic* by Kristeva. Together the semiotic and the symbolic constitute the two modes of signification and are aligned with feminine and masculine libidinal energy which are both aspects of the bisexual individual, even if this bisexuality is repressed. All signification incorporates both modes to some degree, but the semiotic, which has its origins in the pre-symbolic, pre-Oedipal is heavily repressed. The repression of the feminine by the phallocentric organization of the drives on the resolution of the Oedipus and castration complexes gives rise to what Kristeva calls the unconscious semiotic *chora.* This is the site of *negativity,* from which constant challenges to the subject of the symbolic order and symbolic meanings come.

Kristeva argues that the semiotic mode of signification is seen in the pre-Oedipal infant before repression and in non-rational discourses, marginal to the symbolic order. It is both the condition of existence of the thetic subject of language and the guarantee that that subject will always be a subject in process, only temporarily fixed and refixed in language within the symbolic order. The speaking subject is thus a site of political struggle over the validity of the phallocentrism and logocentrism of the symbolic order of patriarchal capitalism. The semiotic, feminine aspect of signification, Kristeva argues, can put into question the stability and apparent permanence of economic and social structures.[5]

It is Kristeva's theory of the subject as unstable, in process and constituted in language which is of most interest to a feminist poststructuralism. This radical alternative to the humanist view of subjectivity, in which it is self-present, unified and in control, offers the possibility of understanding the contradictory nature of individuals and of their dispersal across a range of subject positions of which they are not the authors. Fundamental to this view of subjectivity is the concept of the unconscious which remains, perhaps, the most important contribution of psychoanalysis to understanding subjectivity. Yet the question of how feminists might usefully theorize the unconscious still requires attention, since to take on the Freudian and Lacanian models is implicitly to accept the Freudian principles of psycho-sexual development with their universalist patriarchal implications and their reduction of subjectivity to sexuality. The possibility of a theory of the unconscious as an historically and culturally specific formation of repressed meanings, which are not solely linked to a sexually based concept of desire, together with the psychoanalytic model of language and subjectivity, will be discussed further in the following chapter.

The importance for feminism of psychoanalysis, in both its Freudian and Lacanian forms, lies in the challenge it offers to discourses which assume the unified, self-present subject of rationality, and to theories of innate biologically determined sexual identity. The concept of an unconscious and the separation of the psychic structures of femininity and masculinity from direct biological determination are both important. They are stages in the development of a theoretical position from which the cultural meanings of gender, and the forms of subjectivity in and through which they are realized, become open to transformation.

Having said this, it is arguable that the actual theorization of the structure of the unconscious and of subjectivity which psychoanalysis proposes is too intricately bound up with an inevitable model of psycho-sexual development to serve the interests of feminism. To read Freudian theory in symbolic terms, in which the phallic structuring of psycho-sexual development is a representation of the overall patriarchal form of social organization, is to produce a very partial reading, in which the account of childhood psycho-sexual development can at best be metaphorical. One is then provoked to ask why feminists should use this particular metaphor with its severe and negative implications for femininity? To read Freud as an historically specific account of the acquisition of gender, valid for capitalist patriarchy, does not avoid the inevitable patriarchal implications of the theory. To place the origin of women's subordination within the psychic structures through which sexual identity is said to be acquired is to limit its explanation to a realm which is relatively closed to change. Lacan's stress on the social structuring of the unconscious through language provides the potential for the specific material location of the unconscious. However, to achieve this language would need to be looked at historically, in terms of specific discourses with their attendant social practices, which constitute gender and of which psychoanalysis is but one.

Similar problems arise in feminist appropriations of the Lacanian concept of the symbolic order. Since this order is phallocentric, structured according to the law of the father, it represses the truly feminine, defining femininity in patriarchal terms as a consequence of lack. The uncensored femininity of the pre-Oedipal becomes the material of the unconscious and women's only access to the social is through their compliance with patriarchal definitions of what they are. There can be no escaping patriarchy except through a return of the repressed feminine aspects of language. The assumption that true, un-censored femininity is repressed by patriarchy has led psycho-analytic feminists to look to forms of discourse the subjects of which are women who have been historically suppressed or marginalized. These discourses are seen as authentic attempts to defy the patriarchal order and to reinstate the feminine. They include the discourses of women mystics, poetesses, witches and artists. Witches, for example, provide a particularly powerful symbol of women's resistance to the dominant order and their punishment for failure to conform. In psychoanalytic feminist celebrations of the repressed feminine, they have come to symbolize female desire and erotic expression through sexuality, song, dance and an immediate physical sense of their own bodies. The feminine discourses of mysticism, magic, poetry and art, in which women have contested patriarchy, share a rejection of the rationalist norms of the symbolic order and cannot be contained within the realm of patriarchal meanings. It is for this reason, it is argued, that they have been devalued, repressed or marginalized by being defined as evil or insane.

It would seem that the fundamental assumptions of psycho-analytic discourse about how gendered subjectivity is acquired, about sexual difference and the structure and motivation of the realm of language, law and society, offer little space for feminist appropriation. Nor do feminist attempts to rewrite the meaning of psycho-sexual development by concentrating on pre-Oedipal relations and a repressed feminine libido escape the dual problems of women's continuing marginalization within the symbolic order and the reduction of women's subjectivity to sexuality. None the less, psychoanalysis addresses important concerns which other discourses do not. These issues, the structure of the psyche, the importance of desire, the nature of language, representation, sexuality and subjectivity, all require theorization in a way which is historically and culturally specific and open to change. This is no mean agenda for a feminist poststructuralism and these concerns will be taken up and further discussed in the next two chapters.

4

Language and Subjectivity

The belief that the personal is political is one of the founding assumptions of contemporary feminist theory and practice. The personal encompasses both the nature of the individual, whether this be seen as innate or socially acquired, and individual experience of the world. Yet each of these terms, the personal, individual nature and experience cannot be taken for granted without reproducing dominant assumptions about subjectivity, language and meaning, assumptions which have important political implications. It is with these assumptions and more radical alternatives to them that this chapter is concerned.

Much feminist hostility to poststructuralist theories of subjectivity focuses on their anti-humanist tendency. The critical deconstruction and contextualization of subjectivity, individual consciousness and experience, arguably necessary to the process of radical political change, is seen as a way of devaluing people. Anti-humanism as a theoretical position is often confused with being anti-women, especially by feminists whose primary concern is to revalue and celebrate the experience and culture of women. Yet poststructuralism's concern with the discursive construction of subjectivity, with the role of social institutions and the heterogeneous forms of power governing social relations is motivated by a primary concern with understanding the position of individual women in society and the ways in which they are both governed by and resist specific forms of power. This involves not a devaluing of women's experience but an understanding of its constitution and its strategic position within the broader field of patriarchal power relations.

In chapter 2 it was argued that poststructuralism proposes a particular theory of language and subjectivity which is extremely productive for feminist practice. Yet in order to understand fully the usefulness of poststructuralist theory, it is necessary to make explicit the orthodoxies which it contests, to investigate the nature and implications of those hegemonic versions of language and subjectivity which most people take for granted and which underpin our notions of common sense, social meaning and ourselves.

Not all theories assume that language, subjectivity and gender are naturally given. Chapter 3, for example, looked at currently influential psychoanalytic theories which see gendered subjectivity as a construct. The chapter argued that psychoanalytic theories of gender tend to be universal theories which ultimately look to biological sex, either directly or indirectly, to guarantee the structures of individual subjectivity. The degree to which they integrate cultural dimensions and look to historical social relations to explain gender varies. However, in each case, the project is to fix knowledge, to give a definitive account of the acquisition of gender and its meaning and of the part it plays in the constitution of common-sense knowledge and assumptions which are so important for the maintenance or transformation of forms of patriarchal power in our society.

Subjectivity and Common Sense

Common sense has an important constitutive role to play in maintaining the centrality of gender difference as a focus of power in society. The degree to which particular theories of gender can be assimilated into common-sense discourse varies since common sense itself tends to privilege conscious knowledge and experience, more often than not reproducing the liberal–humanist version of subjectivity. It is common-sense knowledge that gender difference is of primary importance, though the reasons used to justify this are varied. Individuals are subject to gender differentiation from birth onwards. Much research has been done on the care and handling of babies and young children to show the degree to which socially appropriate modes of treating female and male children have been internalized by parents. The ways in which norms of gender difference determine conventions of dress, play and social behaviour for girls and boys are familiar, as is the concern shown by parents over too extreme forms of 'deviance' among 'tomboys' and 'sissies'. Why it is necessary to put so much time and energy into establishing difference is another question. Common sense tells us it is natural and looks to science, social science and psychoanalysis to prove this assumption.

It is in language that differences acquire meaning for the individual. It is in language that we learn how to differentiate pink and blue and to understand their social connotations. Language differentiates and gives meaning to assertive and compliant behaviour and teaches us what is socially accepted as normal. Yet language is not monolithic. Dominant meanings can be contested, alternative meanings affirmed. However, the overriding concern of most parents in bringing up their children is with 'normality', the normality necessary for future success in the two privileged sites of adult life, the family and work. This concern with socially defined normality will lead most parents to accept dominant definitions of the necessity and meaning of gender difference.

Whereas most people see gender-appropriate child-rearing and behaviour as a matter of common sense, this common sense, articulated in language, represents quite specific values and interests. We know how girls, boys, women and men should be if they are normal and we draw our common-sense assumptions from a range of sources which propose different ways of understanding gender. While in some cases our assumptions may be fed by reading books on child development, sexuality or the family, the more obvious sources of common-sense knowledge are general education, the media, relatives and friends. For example, the extended family, neighbours and friends play an important part in exerting social pressures on new parents to conform to 'normal' behaviour.

The assumptions which inform common-sense notions of childcare, child-rearing and education relate to particular definitions of what is natural, appropriate, moral or good. They include an emphasis on particular socially defined feminine and masculine qualities, compatible with future sexual definitions of individuals, together with a taboo on pre-pubertal sexuality. If little girls should look pretty and be compliant and helpful while boys should be adventurous, assertive and tough, these social expectations are not unrelated to girls' and boys' future social destinations within a patriarchal society. Common sense consists of a number of social meanings and the particular ways of understanding the world which guarantee them. These meanings, which inevitably favour the interests of particular social groups, become fixed and widely accepted as true irrespective of sectional interests. How this happens will vary from meaning to meaning. For example, a whole range of discourses and social interests consistently promote the common-sense assumption that children need their mothers. But the experience of two World Wars has shown that how and to what degree this ideology of motherhood is promoted depends on external factors.

All common sense relies on a naive view of language as transparent and true, undistorted by such things as 'ideology', a term which is reserved for explanations representing opposed sectional interests. Common-sense knowledge is not a monolithic, fixed body of knowledge. It is often contradictory and subject to change. It is not always necessarily conservative in its implications. Its political effects depend on the particular context in which it is articulated. However, its power comes from its claim to be natural, obvious and therefore true. It looks to 'human nature' to guarantee its version of reality. It is the medium through which already fixed 'truths' about the world, society and individuals are expressed. These supposed truths are often rhetorically reinforced by expressions such as 'it is well known that', 'we all know that' and 'everybody knows' which emphasize their obviousness and put social pressure on individuals to accept them. As common sense changes, 'human nature' has to undergo redefinition and gender is a particularly active site of such change. In the case of masculinity, for instance, 'normal' men have more options open to them in the 1980s than twenty or thirty years ago. Not only are styles of masculinity more varied, there is a current vogue, for example, for a 'feminine' look, but men can involve themselves in previously female spheres such as childcare and domesticity to a much greater degree without risking censure or derision.

The common-sense assumption that language is a transparent medium expressing already existing facts implies that change does not come about in language. Language is assumed always to reflect changes which occur prior to it. While language in the form of different competing discourses does indeed give meaning to events retrospectively, this meaning is not the reflection of an already fixed reality but a version of meaning. This is not acknowledged by expressive or reflective models of language. In these models an assumption is either right or wrong and is guaranteed by the degree of acceptability it has in a society, by the voice of an 'expert' or by the assumed integrity of the experience of the individual who voices it. Common-sense knowledge has to enjoy a large measure of social acceptance and may appeal to a range of social institutions and social discourses as its guarantee, particularly scientific and medical knowledge. Above all, however, common sense tends to appeal to experience as the guarantee of its truth. This may be collective social experience or individual experience. Common-sense knowledge about how to treat babies, for example, may rely on the collective professional experience of mid-wives and health visitors or on the personal experience of family and friends. What is assumed, however, in both cases, is that experience, like the common-sense knowledge which it produces, is fixed, true and a guide to action.

The key distinguishing features of common-sense knowledge – its assumption of the transparency of language and its appeal to experience – rely on a particular understanding of the individual and of subjectivity. This understanding of subjectivity is itself the product of the long development of humanist discourse in Western Europe through which the God-given, socially fixed, unfree subject of the feudal order became the free, rational, self-determining subject of modern political, legal, social and aesthetic discourses. Unless individuals are diagnosed as mad, or place themselves beyond the limits of what is considered socially reasonable and acceptable within the terms of the hegemonic beliefs and assumptions of a society – in Britain, for example, by proclaiming themselves radical feminists or communists – then it is assumed that we can trust an individual's perception of reality and the 'evidence' of her experience.

However, the experience of individuals is far from homogeneous. What an event means to an individual depends on the ways of interpreting the world, on the discourses available to her at any particular moment. For example, the way in which a woman experiences and responds to domestic violence will depend on the ways of understanding it to which she has access. This will involve her self-image and conceptions of femininity and her beliefs about masculinity and family life. If she sees men as naturally violent or herself as responsible for provoking violence then she is unlikely to see it as an unacceptable exercise of illegitimate power which cannot be tolerated. If she sees masculinity and femininity as natural, fixed and not open to change, then domestic violence will be a personal issue which is not a question of politics at all. The plurality of experience ensures that interest groups put a great deal of energy, time and money into promoting certain views of the world. Masculinity and femininity are cases in point. To maintain current levels of patriarchal power it is necessary to discredit or marginalize ways of giving meaning to experience which redefine hegemonic gender norms. These norms must be constantly reaffirmed as part of the large body of common-sense knowledge upon which individuals draw for their understanding.

The meaning of experience is perhaps the most crucial site of political struggle over meaning since it involves personal, psychic and emotional investment on the part of the individual. It plays an important role in determining the individual's role as social agent. It affects both where and how the individual acts and whether her action is based on a consensual acceptance of the meaning and effects of an action, on conscious resistance to them or on the demands of other external necessities. The power of experience in the constitution of the individual as social agent comes from the dominant assumption in our society that experience gives access to truth. It is assumed that we come to know the world through experience. There is little question of experience being open to contradictory interpretations guaranteed by social interests rather than by objective truth. From early childhood we learn to see ourselves as unified, rational beings, able to perceive the truth of reality. We learn that as rational individuals we should be non-contradictory and in control of the meaning of our lives. This understanding of subjectivity is guaranteed by common sense and the liberal-humanist theory of meaning which underpins it.

Feminism and the Humanist Subject

The distinguishing feature of humanist discourses is their assumption that each individual woman or man possesses a unique essence of human nature. Precisely what constitutes this essence varies between humanist discourses, but in classic liberal humanism, which is still the dominant variety, it is rational consciousness. Rationality is shared by all individuals and is the basis of the liberal political demands for equality of opportunity and the right to self-determination. In feminist forms of humanism the central concern is with women's nature and its identity with or difference from the nature of man. Liberal feminism, for example, aims to extend to women an equal measure of the choice and opportunity currently enjoyed by men. It rejects the long-established assumption that men are by nature more rational than women and therefore should have greater access to self-determination and power. In Marxist and radical-feminist versions of humanism, women's true nature is seen as distorted or repressed by the structure of capitalist and patriarchal societies.

Marxism, like liberal feminism, does not distinguish explicitly between the natures of women and men. Like liberalism, the alienated human nature of Marxist humanist discourse is non gender-specific, that is to say gender-blind. Whereas the sexual division of labour involved in procreation is assumed to be natural, human essence is the same for women and men even though they occupy structurally different positions within society.[1] As a theory of capitalist production, Marxism tends to take procreation and the sexual division of labour for granted, theorizing women only in relation to the labour process. This means that it has very little to say on the question of women's nature or patriarchy beyond seeing it as advantageous to the capitalist mode of production. Recently attempts have been made to extend the humanist-Marxist alienation model of human nature to women and to argue that under capitalism women are alienated from their true femininity. This feminist appropriation of humanist Marxism implies that women have a true nature, different from that of men. Language, in the form of capitalist patriarchal ideology, is seen as central to this process of alienation.[2]

Much radical-feminist discourse also assumes a humanist essence of womanhood. It focuses on the nature of true femininity and is anxious to re-evaluate those qualities which are usually dismissed as feminine and which serve to relegate women to the margins of power. The radical-feminist project is not to deconstruct the discursive processes whereby certain qualities come to be defined as feminine and others as masculine nor to challenge directly the power relations which these differences guarantee. It is rather to revalue the feminine which patriarchy devalues as an alternative basis for social organization in separation from men. Language is central to this process since it is in a new or reclaimed language that radical feminists hope to recapture their essential womanhood.

Feminism and Language

The wish to give expression to women's subjectivity is a key motivation behind the current feminist emphasis on the importance of speaking out as women. In its most radical form this position insists that what we say as biological females about our experience is a statement of what it is to be a woman. To see our statements in this way is to assume that biology is the key determining influence on women's language. Differences of class or race become invisible. Alternatively, in a relativization of the radical-feminist stance, many feminists place a strong emphasis on particular groups of women with shared forms of oppression speaking out, for example working-class, black and lesbian women.[3] This position acknowledges that our experience as women is not innate but is determined by a range of forms of power relation. Yet this position, too, requires further theorization if it is to produce insights into the construction of women's subjectivities and experience which can serve as the basis for radical strategies for change.

The practice of speaking out as women can be a very effective political tool, but it requires an awareness of what we mean when we link women and language. Both women's nature and language are open to a range of interpretations which have different political implications. Similarly the link between women and language can be variously understood. In humanist theory, for example, language is an expression of the subjectivity of the speaker. This subjectivity may be authentic and fixed or the product of a false consciousness, variously produced by capitalist relations of production or patriarchy, which is unable to perceive the real oppressive nature of social relations. For feminist forms of humanism, language is an expression of the woman who is speaking as either womanly or alienated subject. Where the speaking subject is essentially womanly, she is implicitly fixed and it is difficult to see how change can come about. Where she is alienated, it is unclear how she can ever escape this alienation. In order to use language as an effective political weapon on behalf of sexual politics, we need to theorize both woman and language in a way that opens them up to political change. We cannot rely on biological femaleness and language as expression, general categories which suppress the social construction of femininity and language as a site of political struggle.

The idea that it is possible to achieve self-expression of oneself as a woman, man or 'ungendered' individual in language assumes an already existing subjectivity which awaits expression. It also assumes that language is a transparent medium which expresses pre-given meaning. In radical feminism, for example, language describes the already existing natural and distorted qualities of female sexuality and of woman as mother. In this sense it is a labelling system. This perspective on language, in which it is a passive tool of communication, locates the problem of political change in the nature of the individual herself and in her struggle to find her true nature. Unless, as in radical feminism and humanist Marxism, the individual is assumed to be alienated from her true nature, or unless she is subject to moral transformation, as in Christianity, there can be little hope of change. Yet even if such change is theoretically possible, it is unclear how it is to come about, even in a separatist context. Liberal humanism tends to place its hope for change in the powers of reason and moral enlightenment, which it sees as key features of human nature. This is a weak hope in the face of hegemonic conservative discourses which deny the possibility of changing social relations by appealing to the essential fixity of human nature. Women, for example, were long prevented from entering education and public life on the basis of the unsuitability of their nature to such spheres and are still assumed to be naturally fitted for particular types of work.

The transparency of language and the fixity of subjectivity, which are central to humanism, are attractive in so far as they offer a degree of certainty about life and apparent access to truth. If meaning is reflected in language and mediated by experience, our knowledge of the world is potentially true knowledge. We can be sure of ourselves and of our relation to the world. Humanism also offers a sense of security to individual subjects. If you accept that your individuality and your femininity are fixed qualities which constitute your very nature, then you are likely to assume in advance what you can achieve. This assumption is guaranteed by your apparently coherent, self-present consciousness. Yet to see the individual as the source of self-knowledge and of knowledge of the world raises some difficult political problems. How, for example, do we account for the complicity of oppressed people with their own oppression?

If as a woman I know that I am naturally unaggressive, emotional, unself-confident, unambitious, caring, tactful and have a strong need for security, and that this means in social terms that my primary location and sphere of influence is the patriarchal nuclear family where I spend my life on housework and childcare, does this mean that I am oppressed? If I make a conscious choice to earn my living by selling the use of my body for prostitution or pornography, am I oppressed? Liberal feminism, with its belief in the sovereignty of the individual, is unable to deal satisfactorily with this question of 'complicity with oppression'. If a woman's choice is based on her free will then it must be valid. Free will is guaranteed by individual rational consciousness, it is not, in liberal-humanist discourse a relative matter.

The liberal-humanist assumption that the individual subject is the source of self-knowledge and knowledge of the world can easily serve as a guarantee and justification of existing social relations. The structural and institutional oppression of women disappears behind the belief that if I as rational sovereign subject freely choose my way of life on the basis of my individual rational consciousness which gives me knowledge of the world, then I am not oppressed. Oppression is ultimately reduced to a subjective psychological state – feeling oppressed. While radical feminism and humanist-feminist Marxism presuppose a distortion of subjectivity by patriarchy and capitalism, the solutions which they offer to this problem, the development of a new separatist women's culture or social revolution on the basis of historical materialist science, imply a removal of politics from the everyday life of most women. The failure of radical feminism and humanist Marxism to address this everyday life has left it open to the hegemony of liberal humanism.

It is necessary to begin to deconstruct the terms of liberal-humanist discourse in order to see what it takes for granted, what it excludes and how we might offer an alternative theorization of subjectivity and language which is more open to radical change. A first question to be asked is where we get our ideas about ourselves and the world from. The liberal-humanist answer to this question is from experience. For liberal-humanism, experience is what we think and feel in any particular situation and it is expressed in language. Experience is prior to language but requires language in order to be communicated to other people. Experience is authentic because it is guaranteed by the full weight of the individual's subjectivity. It relies on what Jacques Derrida calls a metaphysics of presence, that is the conviction that words are only signs of a real substance which is always elsewhere.

The feminist practice of consciousness-raising takes as its object women's experience of our lives. It involves the coming together of women in women-only groups to discuss our lives from the shared perspective that society is patriarchal and oppresses women. Yet this very process of sharing experience with other women leads to a recognition that the terms in which we understand things are not fixed. Experience is not something which language reflects. In so far as it is meaningful experience is constituted in language. Language offers a range of ways of interpreting our lives which imply different versions of experience. In the process of interacting with the world, we give meaning to things by learning the linguistic processes of thought and speech, drawing on the ways of understanding the world to which we have access. Yet it is possible to transform the meaning of experience by bringing a different set of assumptions to bear on it. In consciousness-raising, the first major breakthrough for most women is the possibility of interpreting difficulties, problems and inadequacies not as the effect of individual, personal failings, but as the result of socially produced structures which maintain a division of labour by sex, together with particular norms of femininity and masculinity, and which subordinate women to men. The recognition that experience is open to contradictory and conflicting interpretations puts into question the ideas that language is transparent and expresses already fixed meanings.

The plurality of language and the impossibility of fixing meaning once and for all are basic principles of poststructuralism. This does not mean that meaning disappears altogether but that any interpretation is at best temporary, specific to the discourse within which it is produced and open to challenge. The degree to which meanings are vulnerable at a particular moment will depend on the discursive power relations within which they are located. To subscribe to the provisional nature of meaning is not to imply that it does not have real effects. Whereas in deconstruction language is an infinite process of play and the deferral of fixed meaning, feminist poststructuralism, concerned as it must be with power, looks to the historically and socially specific discursive production of conflicting and competing meanings. These meanings are only fixed temporarily but this temporary fixing has important social implications. Poststructuralism also necessarily questions the sovereignty of subjectivity as the guarantee of meaning. Meaning can have no external guarantee and subjectivity itself is an effect of discourse. If language is the site where meaningful experience is constituted, then language also determines how we perceive possibilities of change. Language in this sense consists of a range of discourses which offer different versions of the meaning of social relations and their effects on the individual. The way in which we interpret these social relations has important political consequences.

Subjectivity in Process

Many women acknowledge the feeling of being a different person in different social situations which call for different qualities and modes of femininity. The range of ways of being a woman open to each of us at a particular time is extremely wide but we know or feel we ought to know what is expected of us in particular situations – in romantic encounters, when we are pandering to the boss, when we are dealing with children or posing for fashion photographers. We may embrace these ways of being, these subject positions whole-heartedly, we may reject them outright or we may offer resistance while complying to the letter with what is expected of us. Yet even when we resist a particular subject position and the mode of subjectivity which it brings with it, we do so from the position of an alternative social definition of femininity. In patriarchal societies we cannot escape the implications of femininity. Everything we do signifies compliance or resistance to dominant norms of what it is to be a woman.

Potential forms of resistance to conventional femininity are wide-ranging encompassing all areas of social meaning. Dress, for example, necessarily signifies and is open to many different readings. The effect intended by the wearer can never be guaranteed, but this does not negate the potential of dress as a site of conscious sexual–political struggle. It is possible, for example, to dress in conventionally feminine ways yet wear women's liberation jewellery, to dress in ways likely to be read as signifying a rejection of current norms of femininity or in accordance with the current conventions of lesbian culture. Not all resistance is conscious. Whereas some women may refuse to take the tranquillizers prescribed by the doctor, others find relief from patriarchal pressures in mental illness, confirming yet another common stereotype of women's nature.

Our sense of ourselves and of our femininity may be at times contradictory and precarious but only a conscious awareness of the contradictory nature of subjectivity can introduce the possibility of political choice between modes of femininity in different situations and between the discourses in which they have their meaning. The theory of subjectivity as a process, for which this book is arguing, owes a lot to developments in psychoanalysis. For this reason it is necessary to return briefly to the psychoanalytic theories outlined in the previous chapter.

The Psychoanalytic Model of the Subject in Process

The psychoanalytic explanation of the precariousness of conscious subjectivity is to see it as the effect of unconscious processes which constantly challenge the apparently unitary subjectivity of symbolic discourse. In psychoanalysis the heterosexual organization of sexuality and gender identity are the motivating principles behind the structures of the unconscious and conscious mind. Conscious subjectivity, acquired in language, is seen as inherently unstable and subjectivity itself as constantly in process. Ultimately all meaning is guaranteed by the fundamental structuring of the drives which founds the symbolic order of social life. It is the repression involved in the structuring of the drives which creates the conditions for unstable, non-unitary subjectivity. The theory of the unconscious is central to the notion of subjectivity in process. Yet it is possible to conceive of unconscious processes which are not reducible to an ahistorical, sexually based structuring of the human psyche but which are much broader in scope and open to historical change. However, before arguing further for this, it is necessary to look in more detail at the psychoanalytic theory of the subject in process.

As was indicated in chapter 3, the concept of the subject in process comes from the work of Julia Kristeva in which it signifies the inherent instability of the unitary subject of rational discourse and the symbolic order. It is a concept which relies on a Lacanian psychoanalytic model of subjectivity and language. It involves a development of the Freudian theory of the unconscious in which rational consciousness is decentred and subject to the effects of unconscious wishes, desires and processes. In Kristeva's work the unitary subject of rational discourse is termed the *thetic* subject and is an effect of the linguistic structure of the symbolic order. The term 'thetic' refers to the assumption in rational discourse of a unified, transcendent, self-present subject which is fixed in a subject–object relationship of which it is the guarantee and which itself guarantees meaning. The division between subject and object is the precondition for rational language and is realized in the syntactic structure of the language system itself with its distinct subject and predicate. Yet whereas rationalism and phenomenology assume a pre-given, transcendent, knowing subject who guarantees meaning, Kristeva insists that this thetic subject is an inherently unstable effect of language.

An individual's subjectivity is constituted in language for her every time she speaks. All rational language is organized in relation to the subject who speaks. The individual assumes the temporary position in language of the thetic subject via the processes of misrecognition defined in Lacan's theory of the acquisition of gendered subjectivity. Yet language exceeds the

boundaries of rationality and the symbolic order. It is also the
material of the unconscious – the site of repressed meanings.
Kristeva rearticulates this point in a theory of signification which
she calls *signifiance*. Signifiance encompasses both the thetic
structure of symbolic discourse and the effects of what Kristeva
terms the repressed *semiotic chora* of language.

The semiotic chora is the site of those meanings and modes of
signification which cannot be reduced to the symbolic order and
which exceed rational conscious subjectivity. It is an effect of the
entry of the individual as subject into the symbolic order and the
repression which this involves. It is a site of what Kristeva calls
negativity, a process of semiotic generation which constantly
challenges and seeks to transform the apparently unitary subject
of the symbolic order. It is manifest in symbolic discourse in
such aspects of language as rhythm and intonation and is at its
strongest in non-rational discourses which threaten the organization of the symbolic order and the stability of its meanings,
such as poetry, art and religion. In these discourses it demonstrates the temporary and unstable nature of thetic subjectivity
and it is a site for the articulation of the subject in process. While
all language is structured by both the symbolic and semiotic
aspects of discourse, rational language marginalizes the semiotic
aspects, in an attempt to preserve the apparent stability of the
unitary subject and thereby to fix the meanings of the symbolic
order. Because the subject is the crucial site of the fixing of
meaning, subjectivity is also a site of potential revolution.

In Kristeva's work, gender in the sense of femininity and
masculinity becomes an aspect of language. Kristeva links
symbolic language to masculinity and semiotic language to
femininity and argues that both aspects of language, the feminine
and the masculine, are open to all individuals irrespective of their
biological sex. The effect of this theoretical move is to break with
the biological basis of subjectivity. However, in making femininity and masculinity universal aspects of language, rather than
the particular constructs of specific historically produced discourses, Kristeva's theory loses its political edge. Moreover, to
equate the feminine with the irrational, even if the feminine no
longer has anything to do with women, is either to concede

rather a lot to masculinity or to privilege the irrational, neither of which is very helpful politically.

In her more recent essay on forms of feminism, 'Women's Time' (1981), Kristeva argues for a subjectivity which is no longer guaranteed by a specific sexual identity. The account in 'Women's Time' of 'conformist' and 'separatist' feminisms – the one in which women are integrated into the status quo, the other in which they reject it for a separatist women's culture – remains psychoanalytic. Both forms of feminism are identified as paranoid counter-investments produced by women's exclusion from the *sociosymbolic contract*. In what she terms a 'third generation' of feminist politics, Kristeva urges a position from which 'the very dichotomy man/woman as an opposition between two rival identities may be understood as belonging to *metaphysics*. What can "identity", even "sexual identity", mean in a new theoretical and scientific space where the very notion of identity is challenged?' (1981, pp. 33–4). For this to happen, the oppositions on which psychoanalysis is founded must be deconstructed. Kristeva argues that the founding separation of the sociosymbolic contract, as identified in Lacanian psycho-analysis, must be recognized and questioned. As in her earlier work on subjectivity and the avant-garde (1984), Kristeva argues that fiction is an important site for this questioning.

To make femininity and masculinity ever-present aspects of language which exceed rationality and are rational respectively is to propose an ahistorical model of language, gender and the unconscious in which actual historically specific power relations between women and men become irrelevant. In order to open up language and subjectivity to history and the possibility of change, it is not enough to analyse discourse in terms of its 'universal' symbolic and semiotic aspects. While these may have a bearing on the social status and power of a particular discourse, status and power cannot be reduced to this single cause. It is important to see subjectivity as always historically produced in specific discourses and never as one single fixed structure. As an effect of discourses which are heterogeneous and often conflicting, the structures of subjectivity within which the individual is constituted as conscious subject vary. There is no one given universal structure of subjectivity such as both rationalism and psychoanalysis propose.

The Kristevan concept of the subject in process – of unitary subjectivity as an inherently unstable effect of language – is important. Yet we need to extend the analysis to include a recognition of different types of historically specific conscious subjectivity and the different unconscious formations which underpin them. These types of subjectivity, implicit in different discourses, are always located discursively in social institutions and practices which constitute and govern subjects. For the power of all forms of subjectivity relies on the marginalization and repression of historically specific alternatives.

Forms of subjectivity which challenge the power of the dominant discourses at any particular time are carefully policed. Often they are marginalized as mad or criminal as is the case with radical-feminist forms of subjectivity in Britain today. If all women were to turn to radical feminism and its strategies of separatism, the patriarchal order would indeed be threatened. Similarly, if all women in Britain were to espouse the cause of the Greenham peace women who are campaigning for an end to nuclear weapons, debate and government policy would have to shift radically. Yet strong relations of power between discourses, forms of subjectivity and interests exist which make such a development highly unlikely. For example, those media with an interest in maintaining the status quo consistently marginalize the Greenham women. The *Daily Telegraph* in its coverage of alleged Soviet infiltration of the Greenham Peace Camp in January 1986 took the opportunity to alienate ordinary women from the Greenham women through a caricature of anti-rational, radical feminism. Commenting on reports of Soviet 'mock ups' of the Greenham camp, the *Daily Telegraph* wrote:

> Unfortunately the Russians are not as stupid as that. They will have studied *Peace News* as well as the stranger, more exotic literature produced by the 'peace women' them- selves. They will know all about the ritual dances, the construction of great webs of coloured wool in which these devotees entangle themselves, the symbolic objects –

flowers, knickers, dolls – they hang on the camp wire, the worship of the Great Earth Mother, the feminist and lesbian rites, the recrudescence of ancient cults of witchcraft far more powerful in their appeal than Mgr. Bruce Kent. (*Daily Telegraph*, 22 January 1986)

Not many women could identify with this caricature, particularly if we admire the Greenham women.

The Discursive Construction of Subjectivity

Different discourses provide for a range of modes of subjectivity and the ways in which particular discourses constitute subjectivity have implications for the process of reproducing or contesting power relations. In order to understand these implications it is necessary to ask what assumptions a particular discourse makes about language and consciousness. While all discourses work with particular assumptions, differences can be seen most clearly where they are made explicit, as in the case of discourses explicitly committed to producing theories of human society and culture. If we take examples of theories of gender, it is possible to see, in general terms, the ways in which they conceive of language and subjectivity and how this affects their conception of the possibilities of social change. In biological theory, for example, language and consciousness are but outward signs of internal genetic and hormonal differences which determine the nature, female or male, of the individual. Within this model of gender acquisition language is merely a coding system which stands for innate feminine and masculine features which find their ultimate rationale in the efficient reproduction of the species. Social life and communication is governed by genetic and hormonal factors which determine the boundaries of what is possible and desirable. In biological theories the structure of subjectivity, whether genetically or hormonally determined, pre-exists language, which expresses it. In sociobiology and some radical feminism, for example, language is expressive of natural femaleness.[4]

Alternatively, in psychoanalytic theory, subjectivity is one with the structures of language which constitute it. However, the linguistic structures of the symbolic order and of the individual psyche in both its conscious and repressed dimensions are organized in relation to a primary fixed signifier of sexual difference, the phallus, which guarantees both the patriarchal structure of the symbolic order in which social life is conducted and particular versions of masculinity and femininity. As was suggested in the previous chapter, the phallocentrism of psychoanalysis leads to a theory in which femininity is defined in terms of lack and biological women are psychologically tied to a particular version of femininity. Once again language is governed by a general principle beyond historical changes in society and culture. Whereas, for example, in sociobiology and some radical feminism, this guarantee lies in a fixed natural order, in psychoanalysis it lies in a fixed psycho-sexual order which founds sociality. While the unconscious conflicts with consciousness and subjectivity is ultimately unstable, this conflict and instability is contained within the psycho-sexual realm, internal to the individual and not cultural in any historical sense. The political implications of both these types of theory are to fix certain norms of femininity and masculinity as natural and therefore not open to change. They take the existence of patriarchy for granted and are unable to explain why patriarchal relations should be the norm except by appeal to natural laws.

In sociological theory and in social psychology, biological make-up competes with social factors in attempts to explain the acquisition of gender identity. Biology and society are factors of varying importance in the acquisition of subjectivity, and language is taken to be the medium through which subjective identity is acquired in social interaction. The assumption that language is a medium implies that social relations are expressed rather than constituted in language. For example, in developmental theory it is assumed that children learn to be girls and boys through the development of gender role behaviour in an interaction between biological and environmental factors. Adults determine a child's gender on the basis of anatomical difference and reinforce different modes of behaviour in girls and boys according to culturally specific gender norms. Language is used to label and reinforce gender specific norms of behaviour but it is not clear where these norms come from. They are taken to be existing facts of life. Their status as social facts tends to render invisible the social power relations which have produced them together with their inherent instability as the interests which they represent are challenged. An example of this is nineteenth-century feminist challenges to Victorian definitions of middle-class femininity which put into question the 'factual' nature of such definitions even where they were guaranteed by 'scientific' facts. In this process the transparency of language was implicitly questioned, even though the battle for the meaning of femininity was fought by feminists, too, on the basis of new versions of 'true' facts.

Within sociology and social psychology, however, the relationship between language and gendered subjectivity remains descriptive rather than constitutive as it is in poststructuralist theory. Where social science deals explicitly with language, as in ethnomethodology and sociolinguistics, speech acts become social facts which can tells us about the nature of the speaker. Ethnomethodology attempts to gather authentic data about social groups from their own 'natural' speech. In feminist ethomethodology, in particular, every attempt is made to neutralize the effects of the power relations existing between researcher and researched. In sociolinguistics women's speech is most often studied in its difference from male norms of speech. This is done either from a perspective which assumes that there is a natural sex-specific mode of speech which women use or in order to relate women's speech to their subordinate social position within patriarchal society. The first of these approaches assumes that biological sex difference has direct implications for language and that women possess a language that is naturally different from men's language. The second approach sees language as related to social structures and the gender power relations which inhere in them. The implications of biological sex for language in this case will be historically and socially specific.[5]

The relationship between language, subjectivity and sexual difference may be viewed as natural and inevitable, as in biological theory, as a universal structural feature of the symbolic order and the human psyche, as in psychoanalysis, or as social and historical in origin, as in cultural theory. Yet however it is understood, the social meanings given to sexual difference are a key structuring principle of current social institutions, processes and practices. How we understand sexual difference determines the type of society that we will find possible, appropriate or desirable. If we understand language to be an inevitable reflection of predetermined structures of gendered subjectivity then the possibility of effecting social change is removed from the realm of language.

The forms of subjectivity open to us will variously privilege rationality, science, common sense, superstition, religious belief, intuition and emotionality. Whereas, in principle, the individual is open to all forms of subjectivity, in reality individual access to subjectivity is governed by historically specific social factors and the forms of power at work in a particular society. Social relations, which are always relations of power and powerlessness between different subject positions, will determine the range of forms of subjectivity immediately open to any individual on the basis of gender, race, class, age and cultural background. Where other positions exist but are exclusive to a particular class, race or gender, the excluded individual will have to fight for access by transforming existing power relations. For example, women have long had to fight for a larger share of educational provision and in so doing have had to challenge the range of subject positions open to them within the existing framework of discursive power relations. Nineteenth-century women had to lay claim to subject positions which implied rationality and physical strength in order to gain access to education. Working-class women and men had to make claims to citizenship and equality of opportunity by insisting on their powers of rationality, morality and sensibility. Like women of all classes they had to discredit the hegemonic belief that they were naturally inferior, but in this case not just to men but to the middle and upper classes. The partial success of this challenge involved a range of struggles over a long historical duration.

Yet the assumption by the individual of a particular form of subjectivity is at the expense of the qualities, structures of feeling and thought offered in competing forms of subjectivity and denied by the one that the individual assumes. For example, if I take on the forms of subjectivity which Catholicism constitutes, I must ultimately subject rationality to belief and endorse a discourse which is fundamentally patriarchal. The process of assuming Catholic forms of subjectivity involves subjection to a range of repeated rites, rituals and practices which constitute and channel the mind, body and emotions of the individual in particular directions. The reliance of Catholicism on faith rather than rationality has its compensations for the individual in the degree of emotionality which the Church's religious practices produce. Yet this emotionality is structured in quite specific ways and directed inwards rather than towards other people or into the social arena of political change.

Within Catholicism there are subject positions which validate and even celebrate particular modes of femininity, for instance, an approach to traditional family life governed by norms of 'selflessness' which imply compliance to and fulfilment of the wishes and the needs of husbands and children, wishes and needs which Catholicism also defines. These subject positions and the forms of subjectivity which they structure imply particular types of individual satisfaction, pleasure and self-fulfilment and deny the validity of others. In the case of female sexuality, for example, sex is defined as naturally heterosexual and procreative and femininity is implicitly masochistic.

As individuals living in a pluralist society in which Catholicism is one discourse among many, Catholic women are exposed to many other definitions of femininity, women's social role, pleasure and self-fulfilment. For instance, feminist definitions of women's sexuality as different from male sexuality and not dependent on it and of sexuality as an important form of pleasure, separate from reproduction, have implications for women very different from the Catholic views of female sexuality. Catholicism is typical of patriarchal discourses in its insistence on the singularity of meaning, including the meaning of gender. In Catholicism the ultimate guarantee of the truth of the discourse is God, the transcendent subject who *is*. The individual gains a stable unitary subject position by identifying with the word of God as read by the institution of the Church and by becoming subject to the meanings and laws of the Church which define both femininity and women's role.

The fixing of meaning in society and the realization of the implications of particular versions of meaning in forms of social organization and the distribution of social power rely on the discursive constitution of subject positions from which individuals actively interpret the world and by which they are themselves governed. It is the structures of discourses which determine the discursive constitution of individuals as subjects. Yet discourses, located as they are in social institutions and processes are continually competing with each other for the allegiance of individual agents. The political interests and social implications of any discourse will not be realized without the agency of individuals who are subjectively motivated to reproduce or transform social practices and the social power which underpins them. Individuals can only identify their 'own' interests in discourse by becoming the subject of particular discourses. Individuals are both the *site* and *subjects* of discursive struggle for their identity. Yet the interpellation of individuals as subjects within particular discourses is never final. It is always open to challenge. The individual is constantly subjected to discourse. In thought, speech or writing individuals of necessity commit themselves to specific subject positions and embrace quite contradictory modes of subjectivity at different moments. It is the need to regulate disparate forms of subjectivity in the interests of existing power relations that motivates the language of common sense. Similarly, opposition to the status quo calls for attempts to unify certain subject positions and political interests, as in the case of feminism.

Yet the individual is never in a state of innocence when faced by a choice of conflicting subject positions. Indeed often the individual is unaware that she has a choice. Insertion into language begins at an early age and always happens in the context of specific discourses governing family life and childhood more generally. Moreover, it is a consistent feature of most forms of discourse that they deny their own partiality. They fail to acknowledge that they are but possible versions of meaning rather than 'truth' itself and that they represent particular interests. Moreover discourse constitutes ways of being a subject, modes of subjectivity which imply specific organization of the emotional as well as the mental and psychic capacities of the individual. After years of socialization and schooling these may prove hard to change. In addition to this, some forms of subjectivity are more readily available to the individual than others and this will depend on the social status and power of the discourse in question.

The nature of femininity and masculinity is one of the key sites of discursive struggle for the individual and we need only look at a few examples of forms of subjectivity widely on offer to realize the importance of this battle. It is a struggle which begins at birth and which is central to upbringing and education. At the centre of the struggle is the common-sense assumption that there is a natural way for girls, boys, women and men to be. This gives rise to a battle to fix particular versions of femininity and masculinity as natural. In the language of poststructuralism this can be described as a battle for the signified – a struggle to fix meaning temporarily on behalf of particular power relations and social interests. The fixing of the signifier 'woman' or 'man' relies on the simultaneous fixing of subjectivity in a particular discourse.

In the battle for gendered subjectivity, reasoned argument has little role to play. At best it acts as a back up and guarantee of assumptions and beliefs. From the perspective of the individual acquiring gendered subjectivity, discursive authority is paramount. The institutional sites of discourse responsible for the socialization of the child, such as the family, the school, religion and the media, function by the authority of what is 'natural' or 'normal'. The guarantee of the authority of a particular discourse will vary from God to science to common sense. The speaking subject, too, who guarantees the truth of an utterance varies but, in the case of children, is usually a recognized authority figure. Where adults are concerned, the authority of the speaker – as 'expert' or 'knowledgeable' – is part of the discursive battle for subjectivity.

Gendered subject positions are constituted in various ways by images of how one is expected to look and behave, by rules of behaviour to which one should conform, reinforced by approval or punishment, through particular definitions of pleasure which are offered as natural and imply ways of being a girl or woman and by the absence within particular discourses of any possibility of negotiating the nature of femininity and masculinity. Academic, medical and legal discourses offer reasoned accounts of the naturalness of the modes of femininity within which the individual is constituted as gendered subject. A scientific, medical or legal guarantee of truth helps create acceptance of the implications of particular discourses but the justification of gender norms always involves unquestioned assumptions. Particular 'facts' are taken as given, for example, that the meaning of biology is natural and has inevitable social implications.

The use of reason, logic and science as guarantees of the naturalness of patriarchal social structures has not been without its effects on the forms taken by feminist resistance to patriarchal beliefs. The recognition that reason is never value-free and that truth is a social construct used to uphold patriarchal interests has led much feminist discourse to reject rationalist strategies for contesting patriarchal meanings. In a separatist move some feminist discourse has sought to offer alternative models of femininity by creating alternative discourses. This can be seen in feminist religion, philosophy, literature and history as well as feminist versions of female sexuality and the meaning of the female body. In each case an alternative version of the truth of femininity is proposed, guaranteed by an alternative source of meaning. The fixing of meaning is necessary for social life, but in allying meaning to true essential non-patriarchal femininity, such discourse inevitably attempts to fix femininity once and for all. A poststructuralist feminism, on the other hand, committed as it is to the principles of difference and deferral, never fixes meaning once and for all. For poststructuralism femininity and masculinity are constantly in process and subjectivity, which most discourses seek to fix, is constantly subject to dispersal.

How, then, is the battle for the 'true' nature of femininity and masculinity conducted in the world around us? It is in common sense and the other discourses in circulation at any particular moment that we are offered subject positions which assume what it is to be a woman or man and which seek to constitute our femininity and masculinity accordingly. They offer us ways of being and behaving and modes of psychic and emotional satisfaction. In order to be effective and powerful, a discourse needs a material base in established social institutions and practices. For example, the way in which gender is understood and acted upon in the context of the nuclear family is central to the reproduction of the sexual division of labour and current norms of femininity and masculinity. Yet the family is a site of discursive battle over 'natural' gender which has direct implications for the nature of the marriage contract and the socialization of children. This battle over family life is not confined to the domestic sphere. It is found in all the social institutions and practices which help to define the family, for example, the law, social welfare provision, marriage guidance, the media and the churches. Yet it is on the terrain of the family that the effects of this discursive battle are realized. Similarly the gender identities and roles offered to children in the educational context are challenged by some parents and teachers. Yet common sense, the media and peer-group pressure are just some of the social forces which work against the realization of non-sexist discourses in education.

Discourses specifying ways of being a gendered subject may merely imply or actually enforce particular forms of behaviour. This will depend on their social power. Whereas the family and the school, psychiatric medicine and the courts, for example, can force individuals to conform to specific forms of behaviour, this is not usually the case. Yet even in these instances there is room for resistance by subjects who refuse to identify with the subject position which they are offered and to which they are forced to conform at least externally. Yet most discourses work on the basis of consent by offering 'obvious' or 'natural' ways of being and forms of pleasure which go with them. Where existing power relations are under threat, however, initially consensual forms of discourse often employ coercion to govern the subjects in question should consent fail.

At any moment particular discourses and the institutions and social practices which support them determine appropriate modes of constituting individuals as subjects, drawing on a range of ways of addressing the listener, viewer or reader as gendered subject with particular assumptions about the nature of gender, pleasure and satisfaction. No representations in the written and visual media are gender-neutral. They either confirm or challenge the status quo through the ways they construct or fail to construct images of femininity and masculinity. In its treatment of sex and gender, the press, for example, concerned as it is (to varying degrees) with information, entertainment and opinion-forming, is most often anxious to distinguish the abnormal or 'unnatural' from the rest of us. In doing so it rearticulates and refixes social values. In its most extreme and popular form the press is concerned with entertainment through sensationalism. Yet what it means to be sensational, to be beyond the norm is never fixed once and for all. Moreover there are particular interests, often termed the 'general' interest or 'public' interest which are at stake in the discursive battle to determine the 'unnatural'. For most of the British press it includes Greenham peace women as well as rapists and child abusers. The 'serious' press, while less reliant on scandal and titillation for its sales, is just as much concerned with fixing the meaning of acceptable gendered social behaviour, be this through its reporting of incidents and issues or its reviews and features. The range of what is acceptable, however, tends to be broader than in the popular press.

The effectiveness of journalistic bids for the meaning of sexual morality will depend on the strength of the individual's investment in the moral and political discourses with which she identifies and in which she speaks. No individual ever approaches a discourse unaffected by the memory of previous discursive interpellations. Yet press articles use specific linguistic techniques to close off possible paths of resistance to the forms of subjectivity and the meanings and values which they articulate. The most common of these is the implicit assumption of a collective subject, we are all the reasonable, moral individuals for whom the text speaks. This is a strategy which it is hard for the reader to resist. She finds herself placed in a position which implicitly endorses the meanings and values of the article as just good common sense or as eminently reasonable. Yet if we look at the meanings of femininity which we are offered, we soon see that they have quite specific implications for social power.

Like the press, the visual and aural media also employ journalistic forms of discourse with their claims to represent truth, objectivity and decent moral standards. Television, radio and film offer a range of documentary features exploring the 'true' nature or the 'real'-life circumstances of individuals and sections of societies. Documentaries may take several different forms, they may be narrative or non-narrative, categorical or rhetorical or combinations of each. The implicit assumption about documentaries is that they show material that has been filmed on location without any prior staging and that under such circumstances the camera cannot lie. Techniques of filming and the immense importance of editing are often forgotten in the authority attributed to the text and the subject positions it offers the viewer.

Also significant, however, are fictive representations of normal sexual behaviour in the media which concentrate on the relations between women and men in the family, at work, in public life and in leisure. The dominant mode for television, radio, film and video drama is realism. As viewers and listeners we are invited to accept what is offered as a slice of everyday life. We are placed in a privileged position by the conventions of realism from which we can see, with the camera or the narrator, all the different perspectives of the individuals who constitute this slice of life with their different norms of social and sexual behaviour. Yet the realist film, soap opera or radio play is not a reflection of 'real' life. It is constructed as a result of a range of conscious and unconscious choices about what is to be represented as normal or deviant and a range of technical devices help to realize a hierarchy of values within the narrative.

Yet in establishing this hierarchy the subject positions which the listener or viewer is offered are crucial. For example, the twice-weekly BBC soap opera, *EastEnders*, which commands the largest television audience in Britain, offers an apparently privileged view of a slice of 'real' life in the East End of London. In this fast-moving serial, the lives of a number of characters are presented along with their often contradictory attitudes to morality, gender and race. The serial centres on Albert Square, its inhabitants and the small businesses which are located there. Family relations, in particular the relations between women and men are central to each episode. The two relatively stable marriages in the serial at the time of writing contrast with a whole range of broken relationships and with relationships in the process of breaking down or being established. Where marriages are stable other family problems with the old and young are paramount. Where relationships are in the process of change their effects on individuals are shown. These are devastating in the case of breakdown or a source of sanctuary from loneliness and unhappiness where new relationships are formed. In each case the assumption is that a stable heterosexual relationship is necessary to a happy or contented life.

The range of issues on which the serial offers us a perspective is wide. It includes: cross-class adultery and its implications for an adopted daughter; a school-girl pregnancy; childless couples; deserted or single women; remarriage; an illiterate unmarried mother turned to striptease; male striptease; homosexuality and black and Asian broken marriages. No wonder *EastEnders* has such high popularity ratings. Even if as viewers we do not consciously identify with the range of characters and their beliefs and values, we are none the less offered a perspective, an understanding of how 'ordinary' people think and behave which will necessarily address the way in which we conceive of relations between the sexes and gender options in Britain today.

Yet realism is not the only form of fictive representation of gender. Other fictions which make no claims to represent everyday life – such as romance, science fiction and utopian novels, plays and films – also propose norms of femininity and masculinity and ways of understanding the relations between the sexes. In the case of romance, for example, this is their main focus of attention. From the classics of the cinema, which fill our television screens several times a week, to the massive industries in magazine and novel romances, we are offered remarkably timeless representations of femininity, masculinity and love. The romantic heroines of the screen and of novels are defined as physically attractive according to the conventions of their day. Comparing the cinema heroines of the last fifty years it becomes clear just how much norms of attractiveness vary and are tied to fashions in clothes, make-up, hairstyle and physical type. The slim, flat-chested, boyish woman of the 1920s and the 1980s contrasts starkly with the buxom heroines of the 1950s. Yet where there are changes in visual norms of attractiveness, the qualities of femininity which these heroines have are more enduring and point to the relative stability of patriarchal interests. It is not that they do not differ, but that they maintain and reproduce certain basic assumptions about femininity and its relation to masculinity.

For the past fifteen years or so feminist writers, film makers and visual artists have attempted to offer alternative modes of subjectivity to their audiences, modes of subjectivity which redefine or re-evaluate the 'feminine'. They range from the celebration of positive versions of femininity to attempts to deconstruct the bipolar opposition of femininity and masculinity as they are currently defined. Much lesbian fiction, for example, constructs subject positions for the reader which question the normality of heterosexuality by offering lesbianism as a more satisfying, less oppressive or more natural choice for women. Novels with a feminist science fiction element, like Marge Piercy's *Woman on the Edge of Time* (1979) or Zoë Fairbairns's *Benefits* (1979) question existing gender norms and the range of subject positions open to women by exploring different possibilities in futuristic societies. In sweeping historical overviews which have tremendous power, other feminists texts explore women's definition throughout the ages of patriarchy and look for new forms of subjectivity in re-evaluations and redefinitions of biological femaleness.[6] While this work stresses continuities in oppression, much feminist documentary work, particularly in film and photography, tends more towards historical specificity, attempting to show how femininity is socially constructed and how at different moments and in different social contexts women are encouraged to identify with different modes of subjectivity which serve specific interests. The film *The Life and Times of Rosie the Riveter* is a particularly effective example of this approach.[7] It shows the effects of a war economy on acceptable definitions of femininity and women's social and economic role and the drastic change brought about by the end of the war and demobilization.

Although a constant battle is being waged for the subjectivity of every individual – a battle in which real interests are at stake, for example, gender-based social power – dominant, liberal-humanist assumptions about subjectivity mask this struggle. Common sense and the liberal-humanist tradition upon which it is founded suggest that every individual possesses an unchanging essence of subjectivity. Consciousness is thought to be a continuous stream rather than the fragmented and contradictory effect of a discursive battle for the subjectivity of the individual. The exclusiveness of the assumption of a particular form of subjectivity, which rules out its alternatives, together with the individual subject's misrecognition of herself as the true author of her thoughts, speech and writing, gives the articulation of subjectivity in language the temporary appearance of fixity. This sense of fixity seems to rule out change.

However, the temporary fixing of meaning is always precarious. From a feminist poststructuralist perspective the battle for the meaning of gendered subjectivity and the many attempts made by conflicting discourses to fix meaning once and for all is doomed to failure by the very nature of language itself. Language is governed by what Jacques Derrida terms the principle of *différance* according to which meaning is both the product of differences between signifiers and is always also subject to deferral. 'Differance' is what makes the movement of signification possible and ensures that meaning can never be fixed (Derrida, 1973, p. 142).

Even when the principles of 'différance' are inscribed in an historically specific account of discourses, signifiers remain plural and the possibility of absolute or true meaning is deferred. The precariousness of any attempt to fix meaning which involves a fixing of subjectivity must rely on the denial of the principles of difference and deferral. The assertion of 'truth' involved is constantly vulnerable to resistance and the redefinition of meaning. From this point of view particular versions of feminity or masculinity are never inevitable. As individuals we are not the mere objects of language but the sites of discursive struggle, a struggle which takes place in the consciousness of the individual. In the battle for subjectivity and the supremacy of particular versions of meaning of which it is part, the individual is not merely the passive site of discursive struggle. The individual who has a memory and an already discursively constituted sense of identity may resist particular interpellations or produce new versions of meaning from the conflicts and contradictions between existing discourses. Knowledge of more than one discourse and the recognition that meaning is plural allows for a measure of choice on the part of the individual and even where choice is not available, resistance is still possible.

A poststructuralist position on subjectivity and consciousness relativizes the individual's sense of herself by making it an effect of discourse which is open to continuous redefinition and which is constantly slipping. The reassurance and certainty of humanism, with its essence of subjectivity disappears, but so does the inevitability of particular forms of subjectivity with their attendant modes of consciousness. However, to see subjectivity as a process, open to change, is not to deny the importance of particular forms of individual subjective investment which have all the force of apparently full subjectivity for the individual and which are necessary for our participation in social processes and practices. Nor is it to imply that the material structures such as the family, education and the work process, which constitute and discipline our sense of ourselves both conscious and unconscious, can be changed merely at the level of language. Discursive practices are embedded in material power relations which also require transformation for change to be realized. It is the material power relations which constitute and inhere within discursive practices and with the possibilities of resistance that the next chapter is concerned.

5

Discourse, Power and Resistance

This chapter looks at poststructuralist theory of discourse, power and resistance, and its implications for feminism. It discusses how poststructuralist theory can produce politically useful understanding of the production and reproduction of patriarchal forms of power, both institutionally and for individual women and men. It also considers the relationship between poststructuralism and those aspects of contemporary feminist theory and politics which are apparently antithetical to it.

Foucault's Theory of Discourse

It is in the work of Michel Foucault that the poststructuralist principles of the plurality and constant deferral of meaning and the precarious, discursive structure of subjectivity have been integrated into a theory of language and social power which pays detailed attention to the institutional effects of discourse and its role in the constitution and government of individual subjects. For example, Foucault has produced detailed historical analyses of the ways in which power is exercised and individuals governed through psychiatry, the penal system and the discursive production and control of sexuality.[1] Foucault's theory insists on historical specificity. Analysis must look to the specific detail of the discursive field which constitutes madness, punishment or sexuality, in order to uncover the particular regimes of power and knowledge at work in a society and their part in the overall production and maintenance of existing power relations. Fixed, universal meanings of madness or sexuality cannot be abstracted from history. Their meanings always take the forms defined for them by historically specific discourses.

Discourses, in Foucault's work, are ways of constituting knowledge, together with the social practices, forms of subjectivity and power relations which inhere in such knowledges and the relations between them. Discourses are more than ways of thinking and producing meaning. They constitute the 'nature' of the body, unconscious and conscious mind and emotional life of the subjects which they seek to govern. Neither the body nor thoughts and feelings have meaning outside their discursive articulation, but the ways in which discourse constitutes the minds and bodies of individuals is always part of a wider network of power relations, often with institutional bases. Foucault points to the way in which women's bodies were given meaning by and became subject to modern science from the beginning of the eighteenth century onwards. They were, he argued, subject to a process of *hysterization*, made into nothing but wombs, and simultaneously made 'nervous',

> a threefold process whereby the feminine body was analyzed – qualified and disqualified – as being thoroughly saturated with sexuality; whereby it was integrated into the sphere of medical practices, by reason of a pathology intrinsic to it; whereby, finally, it was placed in organic communication with the social body (whose regulated fecundity it was supposed to ensure), the family space (of which it had to be a substantial and functional element), and the life of children (which it produced and had to guarantee, by virtue of a biologico-moral responsibility lasting through the entire period of the children's education): the Mother, with her negative image of 'nervous woman', constituted the most visible form of this hysterization. (Foucault, 1981, p. 104)

This discursive production of the nature of women's bodies was central to the reconstitution of social norms of femininity, the patriarchal subjection of women and their exclusion from most aspects of public life.

The most powerful discourses in our society have firm institutional bases, in the law, for example, or in medicine, social welfare, education and in the organization of the family and work. Yet these institutional locations are themselves sites of contest, and the dominant discourses governing the organization and practices of social institutions are under constant challenge. For example, in Britain today, the role of social welfare provisions in defining the 'nature' of the unemployed and how they should be treated is a site of contest between the competing interests of punitive and compassionate welfare provision. Similarly, the implications of social welfare policies for women, as wives and mothers and as 'autonomous', liberal-humanist individuals is another site of contradiction. The lack of discursive unity and uniformity on these questions means that the individuals whom social welfare policies seek to govern have available to them, at least potentially, the discursive means to resist the implications of existing social policies. Moreover, particular discourses themselves offer more than one subject position. While a discourse will offer a preferred form of subjectivity, its very organization will imply other subject positions and the possibility of reversal.

Reverse discourse enables the subjected subject of a discourse to speak in her own right. In *The History of Sexuality, Volume One* (1981), Foucault gives the example of the discursive production of homosexuality as a subject position, rather than merely a mode of sexual behaviour, open to everyone, a shift which occured in the course of the nineteenth century:

> There is no question that the appearance in nineteenth-century psychiatry, jurisprudence, and literature of a whole series of discourses on the species and subspecies of homosexuality, inversion, pederasty, and 'psychic her-maphrodism' made possible a strong advance of social controls into this area of 'perversity'; but also made possible the formation of a 'reverse' discourse: homosexuality began to speak in its own behalf, to demand that

its legitimacy or 'naturality' be acknowledged, often in the
same vocabulary, using the same categories by which it was
medically disqualified. (p. 101)

Reverse discourse has important implications for the power of
the discourse which it seeks to subvert. As a first stage in
challenging meaning and power, it enables the production of
new, resistant discourses. For example, recent North American
feminist appropriations of traditionally feminine, devalued
subject positions characterized by emotion, intuition and an
abandonment or redefinition of rationality have become the
basis of radical-feminist discourse which has had an important
impact on British feminism. Separatist political strategies have
potentially profound implications for heterosexist patriarchy.
Radical feminism, however, in reversing dominant values, runs
parallel to hegemonic discourse and has yet to subvert its power.
For this subversion to occur it would be necessary for radical
feminist ideas to challenge successfully a whole range of practices
and forms of subjectivity guaranteed by institutions such as the
family, the law, the work process and the education system.

Discourses do not exist in simple 'bipolar' relations of power
and powerlessness. They are 'tactical elements or blocks
operating in the field of force relations' (Foucault, 1981, p. 101).
These 'force relations' are relations of power which take specific
forms in particular societies, organized, for example, through
relations of class, race, gender, religion and age. The field of
force relations includes social institutions, which are the site of
discursive conflict over how subjectivities and social relations
should be constituted and social control exercised. This conflict
has important implications for the ways in which individuals are
constituted and governed as subjects.

Not all discourses have the social power and authority which
comes from a secure institutional location. Yet, in order to have
a social effect, a discourse must at least be in circulation. Much
feminist discourse is, for example, either marginal to or in direct
conflict with dominant definitions of femininity and its social
constitution and regulation. Yet even where feminist discourses
lack the social power to realize their versions of knowledge in

institutional practices, they can offer the discursive space from which the individual can resist dominant subject positions. The possibility of resistance is an effect of the processes whereby particular discourses become the instruments and effects of power: 'Discourse transmits and produces power; it reinforces it but it also undermines and exposes it, renders it fragile and makes it possible to thwart it. In like manner, silence and secrecy are a shelter for power, anchoring its prohibitions, but they also loosen its hold and provide for relatively obscure areas of tolerance' (Foucault, 1981, p. 101). Resistance to the dominant at the level of the individual subject is the first stage in the production of alternative forms of knowledge or where such alternatives already exist, of winning individuals over to these discourses and gradually increasing their social power.

The degree to which marginal discourses can increase their social power is governed by the wider context of social interests and power within which challenges to the dominant are made. It may well take extreme and brave actions on the part of the agents of challenge to achieve even small shifts in the balance of power. This was the case with the suffrage movement in the years leading up to the First World War. Where radical demands can be appropriated, contained or even realized without affecting dominant interests too greatly, change is likely to be easier to achieve. For instance, the principle of equality of opportunity for women and men in education and work, once established, has not proved any great threat to the balance of power in a society where patriarchal relations inform the very production and regulation of female and male subjects. It is possible for liberal discourses of equality to work against women's interests and it is only by looking at a discourse *in operation*, in a specific historical context, that it is possible to see whose interests it serves at a particular moment.

Discourse and Subjectivity

Discourses exist both in written and oral forms and in the social practices of everyday life. They inhere in the very physical layout of our institutions such as schools, churches, law courts and houses. Some may be part of common sense, some may be dormant in libraries or stately homes, their historical moment past, or yet to come. To be effective, they require activation through the agency of the individuals whom they constitute and govern, in particular ways, as embodied subjects. The discursive constitution of subjectivity addresses and constitutes the individual's mind, body and emotions. Subjectivity is most obviously the site of the consensual regulation of individuals. This occurs through the identification by the individual with particular subject positions within discourses. But the discursive constitution of subjectivity is much more than this. It is a constantly repeated process, which begins at birth and is repeated continually throughout life, and which has implications for the unconscious as well as the consciously remembered subjectivity of the individual human agent. Discourses, as realized in institutional practices, for example, in the family and the school, constitute the meaning of the physical body, psychic energy, the emotions and desire, as well as conscious subjectivity. They define individual identities and the forms of pleasure derived from them. Moreover, the acquisition of modes of subjectivity involves the accumulation of the memory, conscious or unconscious, of subject positions and the psychic and emotional structures implicit in them.

Liberal humanism, which is still the dominant discourse in Western societies, assumes the unitary nature of the subject and conscious subjectivity. It insists on establishing the appearance of unity from moments of subjectivity which are often contradictory. To be inconsistent in our society is to be unstable. Yet the appearance of the unitary subject, based as it is on primary structures of misrecognition of the self as authorial source of meaning, is precarious, easily disrupted and open to change.

Subjectivity works most efficiently for the established hierarchy of power relations in a society when the subject position, which the individual assumes within a particular discourse, is fully identified by the individual with her interests. Where there is a space between the position of subject offered by a discourse and individual interest, a resistance to that subject position is produced. Such resistances are a frequent feature, for example, of women's writing in our patriarchal society. The discursive constitution of subjects, both compliant and resistant, is part of a wider social play for power.

Discourse and Power

Power in Foucault's writing is defined as

> the multiplicity of force relations immanent in the sphere in which they operate and which constitute their own organisation; as the process which, through ceaseless struggles and confrontations, transforms, strengthens or reverses them; as the support which these force relations find in one another, thus forming a chain or a system, or on the contrary, the disjunctions and contradictions which isolate them from one another; and lastly, as the strategies in which they take effect, whose general design or institutional crystallization is embodied in the state apparatus, in the formulation of the law, in the various social hegemonies. (1981, p. 92)

Power is a relation. It inheres in difference and is a dynamic of control and lack of control between discourses and the subjects, constituted by discourses, who are their agents. Power is exercised within discourses in the ways in which they constitute and govern individual subjects. For example, the recent spate of attacks in East London on Asian families and their property, is seen by the victims as racist violence. For a long time the police have played down the racial element, choosing to look at incidents in isolation and to avoid the necessity of addressing the issue of racial violence among white youth in a coherent way. The Asian victims do not accept this account of their experience or the policing strategy which it legitimates. However, in this situation, power lies with the police. Yet, the racist complacency of the police and the public at large has led to resistant moves by the Asian community in the form of vigilante groups, which aim to protect Asians but, in doing so, challenge the law. In breaking the law they put its morality, and Britain's claims to being a 'free' society, into question.

Power also structures relations between different subjects within or across discourses. For example, in the nineteenth century, the law defined married women as the property of their husbands, denying them the benefits of legally constituted, autonomous subjectivity. This meant that, in order to be heard, married women were forced to produce alternative forms of power and resistance. Their strategies included the assumption of male pseudonyms and manipulation from 'behind the throne', but both these strategies denied them any voice of their own. Many frustrated women, trapped within unhappy marriages, turned to negative protests, such as illness. The law meant that, in so far as they escaped the modes of government of their subjectivity extended to their married sisters, single women of property posed a problem for patriarchy. By living out alternatives these women threatened the naturalness of the patriarchal family, producing a contradiction the patriarchal resolution of which was a common theme of Victorian fiction.

While Foucault takes power relations to be an always-present structural feature of human societies, his theory does not prescribe what forms power will take in any particular society or area of social concern. Unlike Marxism, for example, Foucault does not begin his analyses with the presupposition that the economic mode of production will be the ultimate determining factor and that, in this sense, class relations and class power are primary. This does not mean that a Foucauldian perspective fails to address the forms taken by economic power relations and their importance in maintaining social power. It is simply that the specific forms taken by economic power relations in any analysis cannot be specified in advance. This form of analysis denies the analyst or the reader the security of knowing in advance how to read and measure power. The certainty offered by a Marxist, liberal-humanist or psychoanalytic perspective is missing.

Power and the Plurality of Meaning

The analyses produced by this theory of discourse are, like their Marxist or liberal alternatives, a *version* of history, which seeks to explain the relations and forces of power from the discursive evidence available. It is a version centrally concerned with the social interests inherent in particular ways of governing subjects and, as such, has important political implications for the present. The process of analysis involves the production of what is itself a discourse on power, which is never definitive and is always shaped by the concerns of the moment in which it is produced. The knowledge inscribed in this discourse implies certain assumptions about meaning which are part of the broader discursive battle over knowledge and power.

If we take, for example, Foucault's text *I, Pierre Rivière* (1978), this point becomes clearer. *I, Pierre Rivière* deals with the case of Pierre Rivière, the son of a Calvados peasant who, in 1835, killed his mother, sister and brother with a pruning bill. The text looks at the documents surrounding the case, including a memoir, produced by Rivière himself, in which he relates the story of his life, and the killings, up to the time of his arrest. The notes which follow the historical material offer readings of both individual sets of documents, and of the event as a whole. These readings, produced in the light of 'a century and a half of accumulated and reconstituted knowledge' (Foucault, 1978, p. 199), are concerned with the relationship between discourse, subjectivity and social power.

In the analysis of the discourses to which the killings give rise, Rivière's deed is seen in the context of the many violent acts perpetrated in the French countryside at that time. Extreme acts of violence, however, were not confined to the peasantry, but could be seen on the world stage of politics and war. Rivière's deed is interpreted as a protest against the intolerable conditions of everyday life in the French countryside, in which poverty, disease and exploitation deprived the peasants of their humanity, of their legally guaranteed claim to autonomous, rational subjecthood. Rivière, it is argued, was making a bid to speak out through his deed: 'By it and in it and after it he would be able to speak the truth and, as a monster, display in their monstrous light the rule of lies and the foul machine at whose whim his fellows, the disinherited of the earth, are and have always been crushed, each day, each life' (p. 177). That it should be necessary to speak through violence is a result of the historical context, which is marked by the frustrated belief of the peasantry that, with the collapse of the feudal order, they had gained 'equality of rights, status as citizens' (p. 179). In effect there had been a shift in the exercising of social power to a system of contracts between individuals.

Pierre Rivière is interpreted as a questioner of the system without the right to speak. Although, legally, feudalism had been abolished, the peasants were still perceived as monsters by other social groups. Their legal equality produced a moment of acute contradiction visible in 'the disarray in the customarily secure and composed discourses of the lawyers and doctors caused by these fine and tragic monstrosities' (p. 183). Rivière's deed is not only a bid to speak, but, in speaking, to change the social power relations in which the exclusion of the peasantry from the social nexus and the failure to grant them a positive position within liberal-humanist discourse, led to their occupying no social position at all: 'The only possibility left him was a reversal of values. Only to those who are excluded from the social nexus comes the idea of raising a question about the limits of human nature' (p. 187). The notes argue further that, under feudalism, higher social status was guaranteed, like the inferiority of the peasantry, by the divine right of kings. In the new bourgeois era all citizens were legally equal and violent crimes of parricide, infanticide and cannablism reflected on the whole society and on what it was to be human.

Much of the analysis concentrates on the discursive battle over the meaning of the killings. Foucault and his collaborators distinguish 'four sets of discourses: Pierre Rivière's memoir and the substance of his interrogations by the examining judge, the dispositions collected from witnesses by the judicial authorities, the medical opinion by Dr. Vastel and his Paris colleagues, and the legal documents drawn before the end of the proceedings'.

Their analysis aims to identify 'shifts in meaning and in the contradictions among and within these four' (p. 229). The results of this battle for meaning determine Pierre Rivière's fate: execution or committal. The analysis of the discourses shows clearly how the different elements available are selectively read or ignored in order to produce readings of the act and memoir as either monstrously evil or insane. Moreover, those elements which are used to found the legal case are played down in the medical case and vice versa. In order to achieve a consistent argument, both are silent on the contents and argument of the memoir itself. It eludes either classification and any serious consideration of it would undermine both the legal and medical cases. It is reduced to silence, taken as a manifestation of monstrosity or of madness. This silencing of the memoir renders it politically ineffectual. The only satisfactory way of silencing it, however, is by declaring Rivière insane, since to have him sane and monstrous would reflect on the common humanity of a society in which all were ostensibly equal. While Rivière is eventually committed, his suicide in prison is taken as a final statement that a reading of his deed and memoir in terms of insanity is inadequate.

The reading which the notes produce relies on a broad analysis of the historical context, the state of the peasantry and of the institutions of the law, medicine and politics, which stresses the unevenness in the social and economic shifts which mark the transition from feudalism to the bourgeois era. While it is but a version of this history, it is one with much explanatory power, showing the implications of the contest between discourses and interests over meaning for individual groups and classes and the effects of silencing on a class which had been led to believe that it now had a right to be heard.

The Case of Sexuality

It is in Foucault's historical studies that poststructuralist discourse theory can best be seen in operation. *Discipline and Punish* (1979a), which deals with the penal system and *The*

History of Sexuality (*Volume One*, 1981; *Volume Two*, 1986) are, like *I, Pierre Rivière*, versions of history. However, the first volume of *The History of Sexuality* offers a clear and accessible account of Foucault's theoretical method. In the following section attention is focused on this text, though reference is made to other texts where they help to illustrate the point in question. (Unless otherwise stated page references refer to *The History of Sexuality, Volume One* (1981).)

In *The History of Sexuality* Foucault defines his objective as an analysis of the discourses of sex and their implications for the constitution and government of the sexual subject:

> What is at issue, briefly, is the overall 'discursive fact', the way in which sex is 'put into discourse'. Hence too, my main concern will be to locate the forms of power, the channels it takes, and the discourses it permeates in order to reach the most tenuous and individual modes of behaviour, the paths that give it access to the rare or scarcely perceivable forms of desire, how it penetrates and controls everyday pleasure – all this entailing effects that may be those of refusal, blockage and invalidation, but also of incitement and intensification: in short, the 'polymorphous techniques of power'. (p. 11)

The objective of *The History of Sexuality* is to 'define the regime of power–knowledge–pleasure' sustaining the discourse on human sexuality in the West (p. 11). The analysis is concerned with the ways in which social power relations are produced and sustained in the discursive production of historically specific sexuality, the subjects which it constitutes and governs, and the emergence of resistance to this power. Sexuality is seen as a primary locus of power in contemporary society, constituting subjects and governing them by exercising control through their bodies:

> We, on the other hand, are in a society of 'sex', or rather a society 'with a sexuality': the mechanisms of power are addressed to the body, to life, to what causes it to

proliferate, to what reinforces the species, its stamina, its ability to dominate, or its capacity for being used. Through the themes of health, progeny, race, the future of the species, the vitality of the social body, power spoke *of* sexuality and *to* sexuality; the latter was not a mark or a symbol, it was an object and a target. (p. 147)

The body is central to Foucault's analysis. He is concerned not only with how bodies have been perceived, given meaning and value, but with 'the manner in which what is most material and most vital in them has been invested' (p. 152). In the modern period, Foucault argues, sex has become a focal point of the exercise of power through the discursive constitution of the body. Yet sex does not exist outside of its realization in discourses of sexuality. Like the signifier in language, it is always historically and socially specific and its meaning is a site of constant struggle. Sex has no essential nature or meaning.

The centrality of sexuality as a locus of power in the modern age has meant that sex has become a focal point in subjective identity. Indeed, it is often found to be the explanation for everything to do with the individual (p. 78). *The History of Sexuality* moves away from what Foucault identifies as the dominant, repressive hypothesis which makes the prohibition of sex 'the basis and constituent element' from which to write a history of sexuality, the fixed point of reference in relation to which all discourse can be read. Instead of privileging repression in the production of a history of sexuality, Foucault argues that a detailed historical analysis points in a different direction towards an expansion of discourses on sex, a 'dissemination and implantation of polymorphous sexualities' through the development of a science of sexuality. This leads to 'a policing of sex: that is, not the rigour of a taboo, but the necessity of regulating sex through useful and public discourses', based on an institutional incitement to speak about it (p. 25).

To speak is to assume a subject position within discourse and to become *subjected* to the power and regulation of the discourse. Foucault argues that for the West, the confessional mode, developed within Catholicism, is the form which this power most often takes. The confessional mode has become fundamental to 'scientific' investigation and knowledge. This mode of putting sex into discourse involves its particular constitution along specific lines to particular ends. The Christian pastoral, for example, 'sought to produce specific effects on desire, by the mere fact of transforming it – fully and deliberately – into discourse: effects of mastery and detachment, to be sure, but also an effect of spiritual reconversion, of turning back to God, a physical effect of blissful suffering from feeling in one's body the pangs of temptation and the love that resists it' (p. 23). Confession played an important part in the constitution and effective government of the Christian subject. The confessional mode implies specific relations of power in which the 'speaking subject is also the subject of the statement', subjected to the discourse which she speaks (p. 61). The questioner is an authority figure who solicits and passes judgement on the confession. Foucault argues that these relations of power have subsequently been transferred to other more recent discourses which often utilize the confessional mode to define and constitute sexuality – for example, medicine, psychiatry, psycho-analysis, ethics, pedagogy, demography, biology and political science. In each case the subject of the discourse is at once constituted by it, and subjected to it, and she has her position as subject guaranteed by the 'expert' enquiring voice. Foucault argues that this mode of discourse has become the principal mode of the science of sexuality which, in the Western world, fills the space occupied by an *ars erotica* in other cultures.

In the development of the science of sexuality, the 'legitimate couple, with its regular sexuality had a right to more discretion' (p. 38). Attention was meanwhile extended to new groupings:

children, mad men and women and criminals; the sexuality of those who did not like the opposite sex; reveries, obsessions, petty manias, or great transports of rage. It was time for all these figures, scarcely noticed in the past, to step forward and speak, to make the difficult confession of what they were. No doubt they were condemned all the same; but they were listened to; and if regular sexuality happened to be questioned once again, it was through a reflux movement, originating in these peripheral sexualities. (pp. 38–9)

This discursive dispersion of the sexual subject brought about both an increase in forms of control over individuals and what Foucault called 'a sensualization of power and a gain of pleasure' (p. 44). The exercising of power itself is a source of pleasure for both its agents and its subjects. Yet, if this is the case, then we need to understand why power is not understood in this diffuse way, but only as a repressive force.

Foucault offers 'a general and tactical reason that seems self-evident: power is tolerable only on condition that it mask a substantial part of itself. Its success is proportional to its ability to hide its own mechanisms' (p. 86). This explanation is compatible with the specific constitution of the individual subject within liberal-humanist discourse, a point which Foucault develops more fully in his text on the penal system, *Discipline and Punish* (1979a). Liberal democracies, for example, in which the role of the state is ostensibly to provide the conditions for the exercising of individual freedom by limiting excesses, function by means of narrow legal and constitutional definitions of individual freedom which are blind to the deep structures of inequality between individuals. The exercising of power in these societies is, therefore, largely invisible. In *Discipline and Punish* power is shown to take the forms of the surveillance and assessment of individuals, realized in the practices of state institutions, such as prisons, schools, the army and the workplace. These institutions discipline the body, mind and emotions, constituting them according to the needs of hierarchical forms of power such as gender or class. For instance, the day-to-day practice of education and socialization constitutes differences in strength and skills between girls and boys, endowing individuals with specific perceptions of their identity and potential, which appear natural to the subjected individual, rather than as the product of diffuse forms of power.

Foucault offers historical explanations of the development of the understanding of power as repression which look to the specific forms taken by the political transition from feudalism to capitalism, and, in particular, of absolute monarchy to constitutional monarchy and parliamentary democracy. Yet, even though the state appears in hegemonic discourse as a regulating body, limiting the excesses that might harm the freedom of the individual, Foucault argues that its interests and investment in other forms of power are widespread. The state, for example, has an overriding interest in governing the sexuality of subjects and controlling individuals. Often this happens by consent. The discursive constitution of sexual subjects enables individuals to function as apparently autonomous subjects 'capable of controlling the use' they make of sex (p. 26). Yet the constitution of specific sexual subjects also creates the conditions for reverse discourse, enabling 'deviant' and powerless groups to speak on their own behalf, to demand recognition and an acceptance of their naturalness.

From the historical detail of his studies of the penal system and of sexuality, Foucault argues that power eludes the total control of any one centralizing body such as the state. The state is one important force among others:

> There is not, on the one side, a discourse of power, and opposite it another discourse that runs counter to it. Discourses are tactical elements or blocks operating in the field of force relations; there can run different and even contradictory discourses within the same strategy; they can, on the contrary, circulate without changing their form from one strategy to another, opposing strategy. (1981, p. 102)

This type of analysis expands the field of potential political activity in ways which are extremely important for feminism, avoiding, as it does, the reductionism of single-cause analyses. In order to produce knowledge from which to act, we must ask of discourses 'what reciprocal effects of power and knowledge they ensure' and 'what conjunction and what force relationship make their utilization necessary?' (p. 102). The interests which a discourse serves may be very far from those which it appears, at first sight, to represent. Discourses have no fixed referent in particular values or systems of morality. Eugenicist arguments, for example, have been used to support widely conflicting interests over the last eighty years, from women's individual rights to contraception in inter-war Britain, to Nazi sexual policy. Indeed, biological arguments are employed by widely contradictory interests, from radical feminism to the most conservative forms of sociobiology, with their strong investment in the reproduction of patriarchy.

Foucault's analysis of sexuality is able to explain both power and resistance in ways which locate them socially and historically, and which point to how resistance is produced and new discursive positions developed. In breaking with notions of essential sexuality, guaranteed by God, nature or the 'universal' structures of human sociality, Foucault opens up sexuality to history and change. His method involves starting not from some general theory of meaning and power, which will inevitably relate it to a universal signifier such as the phallus in psychoanalysis or the capital–labour relationship in Marxism, but from local centres of power/knowledge, like the sexuality of children or homosexuals. The questions to be asked of sexuality are centrally concerned with the diffuseness of power and the possibilities of challenge to it:

> In a specific type of discourse on sex, in a specific form of extortion of truth, appearing historically and in specific places (around the child's body, apropos of women's sex, in connection with practices restricting births and so on), what were the most immediate, the most local power relations at work? How did they make possible these kinds of discourse, and conversely, how were these discourses used to support power relations? How was the action of these power relations modified by their very exercise, entailing a strengthening of some terms and a weakening of others, with effects of resistance and counterinvestments, so that there has never existed one type of stable subjugation, given once and for all? How were these power relations linked to one another according to the logic of a great

strategy, which in retrospect takes on the aspect of a unitary and voluntarist politics of sex? (p. 97.)

From a detailed analysis of the ways in which these locations of power are inscribed in discourse, it is possible to identify patterns of modification in force relations, which, Foucault suggests, are ultimately part of some overall strategy of power and control, or of resistance to it. Feminists would identity this strategy as, at least in part, patriarchal.

The assumption that sexuality is an historical construct which is the site of 'an especially dense transfer point for relations of power: between men and women, young people and old people, parents and offspring, teachers and students, priests and laity, an administration and a population' makes sexuality an important site for the analysis of power without prescribing the precise importance of sexuality (p. 103). Foucault stresses the need to resist single explanations, which simplify the social implications of sexuality and render much of its power invisible:

> There is no single, all-encompassing strategy, valid for all of society and uniformly bearing on all the manifestations of sex. For example, the idea that there have been repeated attempts, by various means, to reduce all of sex to its reproductive function, its heterosexual and adult form, and its matrimonial legitimacy fails to take into account the manifold objectives aimed for, the manifold means employed in the different sexual politics concerned with the two sexes, the different age groups and social classes. (p. 103)

For feminists, the attempt to understand power in all its forms is of central importance. The failure to understand the multiplicity of power relations focused in sexuality will render an analysis blind to the range of points of resistance inherent in the network of power relations, a blindness which impedes political resistance. Explanations of patriarchy, for example, which seek to account for it only in terms of privileged forms of power such as the capitalist mode of production, the nuclear family or male violence against women, offer necessarily partial, politically limited analyses. Foucault insists that 'points of resistance are present everywhere in the power network' and revolt or revolution have likewise no one reference point (p. 95). While 'great radical ruptures, massive binary divisions' do occur occasionally, 'more often one is dealing with mobile and transitory points of resistance, producing cleavages in a society that shift about, fracturing unities and effecting regroupings' (p. 96). It is from this perspective that we can best address the specific forms of power exercised in society and attempt to contest them.

Discourse Theory and Feminist Practice

Foucault's work has, at times, been received with hostility on account of its anti-humanism, a charge which renders it inimical to important strands within feminism. It was argued in the previous chapter that this charge of anti-humanism, often directed at poststructuralist theory, is generated by its approach to subjectivity. Poststructuralism is seen as denying the authenticity of individual experience by decentring the rational unitary, autonomous subject of liberal humanism, or the essential female nature at the centre of much radical feminism, rendering it socially constituted within discourse. What Foucault's work offers feminists, however, is a contextualization of experience and an analysis of its constitution and ideological power.

Although the subject in poststructuralism is socially constructed in discursive practices, she none the less exists as a thinking, feeling subject and social agent, capable of resistance and innovations produced out of the clash between contradictory subject positions and practices. She is also a subject able to reflect upon the discursive relations which constitute her and the society in which she lives, and able to choose from the options available.

The options available to women in the battle to define our femininity, social role and the meaning of our experience are many. However, they exist in a hierarchical network of antagonistic relations in which certain versions of femininity and the sexual division of labour have more social and institutional power than others. In order to develop strategies to contest hegemonic assumptions and the social practices which they guarantee, we need to understand the intricate network of discourses, the sites where they are articulated and the institutionally legitimized forms of knowledge to which they look for their justification. The most common guarantees of the 'truth' of discourses are science, God and common sense. In the case of biological sexual difference, for example, each of these sources of truth forms part of an overall discursive strategy the effects of which are to conserve patriarchal interests. Biological sexual difference is a particularly intense site of discursive struggle in which our subjectivity is constituted for us in language and social practices which form and discipline our bodies, minds and emotions.

Biology and Sexual Difference:
a Feminist Poststructuralist Perspective

Theories of the meaning of sexual difference can be divided into three broad types: those which appeal to science and nature, those which look to psychoanalytic theory and those which, in various ways, offer social and historical accounts of its meaning. Each of these types of theory has been mobilized, at different times by conflicting interest groups, in the battle to reaffirm or contest the patriarchal power relations of everyday life. While it is possible to analyse their assumptions, the social interests which discourses represent will depend on the specific historical context in which they are articulated.[2]

Biological differences between the sexes, for example, are a major material ideological support and guarantee of patriarchal social structures, from the sexual division of labour and the structure of contemporary forms of femininity, to women's position in society at large. Feminists concerned with theorizing sexual difference are necessarily already positioned within a discursive field of ways of understanding, many of which have profound implications for social processes and practices. The number of discourses which constitute notions of sexual difference is immense, ranging from biological science and psychology to religion and the arts, but present in almost every discourse is the spectre of biology. Theories which reject biological determinism of any kind, at the very least, have to take account of it.

Patriarchy implies a fundamental organization of power on the basis of biological sex, an organization which, from a poststructuralist perspective, is not natural and inevitable, but socially produced. While biological differences exist, the degree to which they are emphasized, and the meanings they are given, vary. For example, sexual difference can be looked at as a fundamental binary opposition or as a continuum which allows for degrees of difference. For poststructuralism, biological differences do not have inherent 'natural' or social meaning. Their meanings, which are far from uniform, are produced within a range of conflicting discourses, from medicine and sociobiology to radical feminism.

Feminist theory must be able to analyse the range of meanings which biological difference has in our society, and the political structures which particular meanings justify. This analysis is not merely an intellectual process. It is a process founded in the day to day practices in which we constantly assume feminine subject positions, and find ourselves subject to definitions of our femininity, often at variance with the ways in which we define our interests as women. The degree to which the meaning of biology is to the fore will vary according to the specific discursive context. It is particularly pronounced, for example, in women's confrontations with and subjection to medical and psychiatric discourses, particularly gynaecology. The frequency with which pregnancy is put forward by doctors as the best cure for specific medical problems leads one to wonder about the conflation of medical techniques and discourses of femininity. The knowledge produced for women through the process of subjection to such discourses can be the basis for the articulation of alternative meanings, which do not marginalize and subordinate women and which, in the process, transform the hegemonic structures of masculinity.

Biological theories of sexual difference attempt to ascribe social definitions of the nature and function of femininity and masculinity to a fixed and unchanging natural order, guaranteed by the female or male body, independently of social and cultural factors. They have a history as long as the social and biological sciences themselves and appeal to biological difference between women and men, both observable and imagined, to explain the naturalness and inevitability of our different social status and function, particularly at times when women have fought for change.

Biological debate has focused on two main areas – identifying difference and interpreting its social meaning. Yet, in practice, these two areas are often conflated. Attempts to identify difference have, as often as not, taken specific, socially and historically produced differences as their starting point. Their arguments are typically tautological, suggesting, for example, that the empirical 'truth' that, in all known societies, women have primary responsibility for childcare, care of the aged and sick, both within and outside the family, demonstrates that we must be naturally suited to these roles. To explain women's nature biological arguments then look for scientific guarantees of 'obvious' facts about women, finding them in a range of theories which appeal to anthropomorphic studies of other mammals, to instincts, hormones or to the physical processes of reproduction. Biological arguments have been used both against and in support of the emancipation of women, and social theories have looked to biological science, and to psychology, for proof of women's inferiority, superiority or, most often in this century, our equality in difference. At the present moment, sociobiology provides an uncompromising example of this type of discourse, which, like social Darwinism in the nineteenth century, continues to feed both social policy and common sense.

Sociobiology is concerned with the effects of biology on social behaviour. It sets out to demonstrate how natural genetic and hormonal differences between the sexes result in different 'natural' forms of behaviour and spheres of activity and influence. Among the most influential examples of this theory is the 'selfish gene' theory, best known in the work of Richard

Dawkins, who published a book of this title in 1976. According to *The Selfish Gene* all human behaviour is governed by the impulse to see one's own genes survive in oneself and one's children. The form that this self-interest takes is sex-specific. The natural differences between women and men are already visible in the meaning which *The Selfish Gene* attributes to the difference between the ovum and the sperm. This is taken to show that women naturally invest more in their children than men and are the primary child carers. Men are genetically given to promiscuity, through which they can impregnate a greater number of women with their genes. In this way, the sexual division of labour and sexual double standards are rendered natural. *The Selfish Gene* is but one extreme example of a type of 'scientific' discourse attempting to fix the truth of women's and men's natures. It is when assumptions, such as these, about what is natural structure the social and institutional practices which constitute the subjectivity, bodies, minds and emotions of girls and boys and women and men, that their power is realized and patriarchal relations reaffirmed. This happens, for example, in education and psychiatry, practices centrally concerned with the constitution of the individual.

If we look historically and cross-culturally at biological reproduction, and its position and importance in the lives of women and men, it becomes clear that concepts of biological naturalness are constituted by social organization, levels of social development and the forms of language in which these are realized. For example, the socially organized, natural processes of conception, childbirth and child-rearing and the position which they occupy in women's lives in the 1980s are very different from previous centuries before industrialization, the establishment of the nuclear family, the extension of childhood and the development of reliable contraception, abortion and infant-feeding formulas. On a smaller historical scale, the significance and degree of exclusiveness attributed to women's familial role has varied, among other things, with the economic pressures structuring the demand for women's labour. In the twentieth century, this has been most clear in times of war, when governments have gone to considerable lengths to attract into the workforce women whose previous identity was that of wife and mother, defined, until then, as incompatible with work outside the home.

The twentieth century has seen the development of the technical prerequisites for Western women to live non-celibate lives, independently of biological reproduction. Yet, in spite of this, common-sense values still insist that women's primary role is in the home. The prevailing assumption that motherhood and child-rearing bring women 'natural' self-fulfilment, and, by inference, that childless women are not quite what they should be, involves attributing particular social meanings and values to the physical capacity to bear children. The 'essential' biological nature of women guarantees the inevitability that we should fulfil particular economic and social functions which may not be in our own interests.

The effect of sociobiology, and discourses like it, is to determine in advance what constitutes normal femininity and masculinity, to fix subjectivity, by insisting that certain meanings are the true ones, because they are determined by natural forces beyond our control. Natural femininity and masculinity necessarily fit women and men for different types of jobs and social and familial tasks. Given the way in which sociobiology fixes meanings, it can only serve the interests of men. It does so by insuring that women and men are defined in advance, and irrespective of individual desires or wishes, as suited to particular ways of life, employment, forms of sexuality and family relationships. The differences between them are hierarchical, involving different degrees of access to the power to determine the nature of society. Where women seek to challenge the assertion which biological theories make about their nature, they are told that they are going against nature itself. Resistance within the terms of this discourse is impossible because it denies women any alternative place from which to speak. Its truth is apparently homogeneous, guaranteed by the combined forces of rationalism and empiricism.

Sociobiology, like much scientific discourse, assumes that knowledge is founded on the empirical observations of a neutral observer who can infer from the particular to the general. The assumption that it is possible to ascertain objective, true facts, and to be a neutral observer, implies that science is independent of particular social and moral values and interests. This position sees language as a transparent tool for expressing facts, rather than the material in which particular often conflicting, versions of facts are constructed. It relies on an autonomous and coherent observing and recording subject, rather than a subject who is herself socially constructed within specific value-laden discourses.

It is on this basis that sociobiology makes its claims to truth. 'Truth' is by definition fixed, absolute and unchanging. It is the final guarantee of the way things are. It offers stability and evades questions of interest, in this case women's or men's interest. Social recognition of their truth is the strategic position to which most discourses, and the interests which they represent, aspire. To achieve the status of truth they have to discredit all alternative and oppositional versions of meaning and become common sense.

Feminism and the Question of Truth

It is in making claims to truth that discourses demonstrate their inevitable conservatism, their investment in particular versions of meaning and their hostility to change. It is possible for feminists to approach the question of truth from within this same discursive framework, aiming, through reversal, to establish new truths, compatible with their interests, and this is a strategy which may, at times, prove politically useful. It has been most apparent in liberal feminism, which has sought equality within existing social relations. For many years, for example, liberal feminists tried to establish that women's physiology did not render them incapable of educational and professional achievement. Attempts to use these discursive strategies to claim the truth of alternative scientific 'facts' about women's nature are, however, unlikely to succeed in radically transforming patriarchal structures and practices. The power relations of the discursive field work against them. The institutional investment in science which confirms the status quo is massive. Feminists do not have the resources or the institutional positions and backing to make much impact on the discursive hierarchy of existing writing and research, backed, as it is, by capitalist and patriarchal interests. Contraception, for example, a multi-million pound business, is a case in point. Women often remark that the known long-term dangers of the pill would not be tolerated if it were prescribed for men. Among the reasons given for not marketing a male hormonal contraceptive is the unacceptibility of side effects, such as loss of sexual libido, which are minor when compared with those of the pill. The social position of women ensures that the minor side effects of the pill and the prospect of health problems in later life, are outweighed, for most women, by the need for independent control of our fertility. Women do not have the institutional and commercial power to insist on research which might result in less dangerous contraception.

Radical-feminist discourse takes a different position from liberal feminism both on the meaning of biological sexual difference and on the possibilities of reforming patriarchal institutions, practices, meanings and values. Its project is to reject patriarchal concepts of meaning, and the ways in which they have defined women. Instead of arguing over the facts of women's nature, countering one set of scientific 'truths' with another, radical feminists, such as the American writers Mary Daly and Susan Griffin, attempt to redefine femaleness by subverting accepted language and conventional rationality and producing new meanings and new subject positions. Mary Daly's *Gyn/Ecology* (1979) is a powerful example of this strategy.

Gyn/Ecology is concerned with exposing the repressive techniques and practices of patriarchy throughout the ages, and with encouraging women to create a new identity for themselves. Women's new identity is founded on 'true' femaleness, based in women's biological nature. Aspects of femaleness are open neither to men nor to transsexuals. The process of achieving a new identity is conceived as a journey, which involves breaking with patriarchal perspectives, confronting the full horror of patriarchy and developing and celebrating new organic female creativity, for which Daly uses the image of 'spinning' in a new space. Daly takes familiar words used to describe women, many of them abusive, such as 'hag', 'crone' and 'spinster', and invests them with new, positive meanings. Similarly she 'unmask[s] deceptive words by dividing them and employing alternative meanings for pre-fixes' (p. 24). Words such as 'a-maze', 'the-rapist' and 're-cover' acquire new meanings. 'A-maze' comes to mean unravelling the maze of patriarchal meanings, 'therapy' becomes a form of rape as in 'the-rapist' and 're-cover' means to cover anew. *Gyn/Ecology* uses images of witches and Amazons to symbolize new female power in which women are linked in sisterhood, self-identified instead of male-identified, totally rejecting contact with men and heterosexuality.

Much of *Gyn/Ecology* is concerned with documenting the horrors of Indian *suttee*, Chinese footbinding, African genital mutilation, European witch burning and American gynaecology, and with the ways in which male scholarship has handled these subjects. At the end of this 'Passage' or section, the focus changes to creating a new female environment:

> Since we have come through the somber Passage of recognizing the alien/alienating environment in which woman-hating rituals vary from *suttee* to gynecological iatrogenesis, we can begin to tread/thread our way in new time/space. This knowing/acting/Self-centering Process is itself the creating of a new, women-identified environment. It is the becoming of Gyn/Ecology. This involves the dis-spelling of the mind/spirit/body pollution that is produced out of man-made myths, language, ritual atrocities, and meta-rituals such as 'scholarship', which erase our Selves. It also involves dis-covering the source of the Self's original movement, hearing the moving of this movement. It involves speaking forth New Words which correspond to this deep listening, speaking words of our lives. (p. 315)

Daly suggests that the new woman-identified environment enables the realization of women's true selves, which patriarchy distorts, fragments and denies. All women are said to be aware, at some level, of their true natures. The true female self is identified with wild, undomesticated nature. Women who have freed themselves from their patriarchal identification are said to 'feel a deep communion with our natural environment. We share the same agony from phallocratic attack and pollution as our sister the earth. We tremble with her' (p. 409). This linking of woman and nature is a frequent feature of radical-feminist alternatives to patriarchy. It is taken up and expanded, for example, in the work of Susan Griffin. She, too, rejects patriarchal language, logic and linearity in favour of a diffuse web of meaning constructed from various discourses, from historical facts and scientific quotations to poetry. Like Mary Daly, she emphasizes the suppression and exploitation of women, drawing parallels between patriarchal treatment of women and of nature. Again the project is to mark women's essential, true difference from men which can only be realized in a new separate space of female creativity.

Gyn/Ecology ends with an image of this new creativity. It is the dawn of a new era, but what this new way of living means in terms of everyday life is left unspecified:

> As we feel the empowerment of our own Naming we hear more deeply our call of the wild. Raising pairs of arms into the air we expand them into shells, sails. Splashing our legs in the water we move our oars. Our beautiful, spiral-like designs are the designs/purpose of our bodies/minds. We communicate these through our force-fields, our auras, our O-Zones. We move backward over the water, towards the Background. We gain speed. Argonauts move apart and together, forming and re-forming our Amazon Argosy. In the rising and setting of our sister the sun, we seek the gold of our hearts' desire. In the light of our sisters the moon and the stars we rekindle the Fore-Crones' fire. In its searing light we see through the fathers' lies of genesis and demise; we burn through the snarls of the Nothing-lovers. (p. 423–4)

This totalizing strategy of radical-feminist discourse, in which a new version of true, biological femaleness replaces patriarchal definitions, cannot engage with the problems and power relations of everyday life. The most it can do is to see them as effects of the patriarchy which it urges women to leave behind. It is a clear example of a discourse without the social and institutional power to effect change, but more than this, it rejects the need to engage politically with the complex power relations of particular patriarchal societies.

By fixing female nature abstractly, in separation from the social practices of everyday life, radical feminism leaves individual women to work out its meaning in their own lives. In practice this means adopting and adapting existing forms of femininity which are historically specific. In the United States, this has taken the form of separatist women's communes in which traditional forms of femininity are privileged, but removed from the service of men. They have the status of a sub-culture, contained within the power relations of patriarchal capitalism.

For poststructuralist feminism, neither the liberal-feminist attempt to redefine the truth of women's nature within the terms of existing social relations and to establish women's full equality with men, nor the radical-feminist emphasis on fixed difference, realized in a separatist context, is politically adequate. Both these forms of feminist discourse are trapped by their attempts to define women's nature once and for all. Poststructuralist feminism requires attention to historical specificity in the production, for women, of subject positions and modes of femininity and their place in the overall network of social power relations. In this the meaning of biological sexual difference is never finally fixed. It is a site of contest over meaning and the exercise of patriarchal power. This discursive contest, in which women can resist particular meanings and power relations, is subject to historical change. An understanding of how discourses of biological sexual difference are mobilized, in a particular society, at a particular moment, is the first stage in intervening in order to initiate change.

6

Feminist Critical Practice

The principles of feminist poststructuralism can be applied to all discursive practices as a way of analysing how they are structured, what power relations they produce and reproduce, where there are resistances and where we might look for weak points more open to challenge and transformation. Particular feminist strategies will depend on the analysis of power relations from within which we attempt change. This final chapter offers the outlines of a case study of one particular institutional practice, literary criticism, seen from a feminist poststructuralist perspective. Feminist poststructuralism demands attention to social, historical and cultural specificity. For this reason the focus in this chapter is limited to Britain and the impact in the British context of other European and American feminist criticism. There will be differences between the forms taken by institutional power and the practices it legitimates in Britain and elsewhere. The forms that resistance and the development of new practices take will also vary. Within these limits this chapter is at once an attempt to show poststructuralist analysis in operation and also to offer a possible way forward for feminist critical practice in literature and cultural studies.

To practice literary criticism is to produce readings of literary texts and in the process of interpretation temporarily to fix meaning and privilege particular social interests. Feminist criticism seeks to privilege feminist interest in the understanding and transformation of patriarchy. How the feminist critic fixes meaning will depend on the framework within which she reads a text. Texts may be read, for example, as expressions of women's experience already constituted in the world beyond fiction, as repressions of an essentially feminine subjectivity which may be heterosexual or lesbian and which seeks to reassert itself through the discursive strategies of fiction or as specific examples of the construction of gender in language. These different types of reading represent different political as well as theoretical objectives.

To read for the expression of women's experience, for example, is to locate the meaning of fiction outside itself in the life and consciousness of the author rather than in the historically placed interaction between reader and text. The author gives expression to her experience and guarantees its authenticity. This way of reading relies on the assumption of a fully self-present female subject, rather than a changing and contradictory subject, such as the subject of poststructuralism, whose experience is discursively produced and constantly open to redefinition. From the poststructuralist position for which this book is arguing fiction offers access to the discourses constituting gender and the meaning of women's lives at the time of writing as framed by the conventions of the literary discourses of the period and read through the concerns of the present day. It cannot be the expression of already constituted experience. However given the wide popularity which experience-based criticism currently enjoys, particularly among American feminists, it is important to look more closely at its assumptions, aspirations and potential. These will be discussed in more detail later in this chapter.

Where fiction is seen by the reader to be concerned with repressed essential femininity, the readings which the critic produces will rely on the assumptions about this femininity which she brings to the text. Often in feminist criticism these assumptions are ultimately psychoanalytic or biological, but however 'true' femininity is conceived, it has important political implications for how we understand gender and future possibilities of change. If we take, for example, the work of Adrienne Rich, where true femininity is tied to lesbianism and to women's creative powers of motherhood, the implications for women are profound. Whatever new values are ascribed to female sexuality and to motherhood, women's nature remains located in biological processes.

Where texts are read as sites for the discursive construction of the meaning of gender, as in feminist poststructuralist readings, their meanings will relate both to the original historical context of production, understood through the discourses which constitute present day conceptions of history, gender and meaning, and to the concerns of the present. For example, Catherine Belsey's study *The Subject of Tragedy* (1985), demonstrates among other things the implications for women of the discursive shifts which brought about the birth of the liberal-humanist, knowing self-present subject and some of the ways in which women resisted their exclusion from this discourse.

Meaning is always political. It is located in the social networks of power/knowledge relations which give society its current form. Not all areas of discourse are equally significant in the hierarchy of power/knowledge relations but no discursive practice is outside them. The position of feminist criticism, both actual and potential, within the broader discursive fields of cultural criticism and sexual politics, is an important question for feminists since it concerns our power to change existing social relations. This chapter looks at feminist criticism as a discursive practice and at its power and potential as an area of struggle in the broader feminist fight to transform patriarchal power relations. It attempts to cover both institutional and extra-institutional practices and textual analysis. It is not a comprehensive review of feminist criticism but an argument for a move into a poststructuralist feminist criticism which puts into question existing institutions and practices and initiates a rethinking of why and how we might study cultural products.

Meaning and Power

As critics we are primarily concerned with producing meanings. All meanings have implications for existing social relations, contesting them, reaffirming them or leaving them intact. The meaning and the social and political implications of a reading will be determined by the position within the discursive field from which the critic reads and the knowledges inscribed in the discourses with which she reads. From a feminist poststructuralist perspective the process of criticism is infinite since meaning can never be finally fixed. Every act of reading is a new production of meaning. Positions from which to read and the discourses with which to read are in principle infinite and constantly changing. At any particular historical moment, however, there is a finite number of discourses in circulation, discourses which are in competition for meaning. It is the conflict between these discourses which creates the possibility of new ways of thinking and new forms of subjectivity.

The institution of literary criticism in Britain has long been at pains to privilege certain types of reading and certain forms of knowledge and social values above others. For the last fifty years Leavisite criticism, with its appeal to fixed moral and political values, the critic as the arbiter of these values and literature as a privileged mode of access to truth through its evocation of 'life' has dominated literary discourse in education, publishing and reviewing. Like the liberal-humanist criticism which preceded it, Leavisite criticism claims to address both the unique individual and the universally human, but in both cases its gender blindness has created the conditions for a discourse which is profoundly conservative and patriarchal in its implications. The individual and the human nature for which it speaks are both normatively male, and the meanings and values which it privileges naturalize the social power relations of patriarchy. Moreover, its critical practice, marked by its appeal to the professional critic as the true interpreter of literature and guardian of the literary tradition, and its authoritarian appeal to value-laden criteria of individual critical sensibility rather than to explicit, learned modes of reading, mystifies the critical process in ways which are totally at odds with feminist criteria of knowledge production.

The appeal of seeing 'great' literature as the receptacle of fixed universal meanings which enable us to understand the 'truth' of human nature, which is itself fixed, has been widespread. It is part of the hegemony of liberal-humanist discourses on subjectivity, language and culture. Over the last 120 years the literary critic has had an important ideological role in Britain as the guardian of meanings and values which, while ostensibly literary and therefore non-partisan, are informed by assumptions about class, gender and race. From Matthew Arnold onwards, sections of the literary establishment have seen in culture and more specifically in literature, carefully selected and properly read, a force to combat social unrest and to silence calls for revolutionary change in the broader power structures of society. From the 1860s until the 1920s the 'national literature' was seen as the basis for a common culture which would unite all classes in supposedly shared interests, and as recently as 1981 Lord Scarman, who chaired the enquiry into the Brixton riots in London, urged the acquisition of a common language and culture as a solution to racial violence, a common culture defined by a white middle-class elite.

To speak of the institution of literary criticism is to draw together a range of institutional sites and practices which between them give the discursive field of literary criticism its hegemonic aspects. It is in the universities, in state cultural institutions, in publishing, in reviewing, in the awarding of literary prizes and in all branches of education that critical practices are established, reproduced and challenged. Yet the hierarchy of literary values, literary discourses and practices most often justified in the name of 'excellence', the 'national heritage' and the 'great tradition' is but part of the discursive field. This also includes oppositional moves to challenge the hegemonic, hierarchical system of exclusions of feminist, non-white, non-heterosexual and non middle-class interests, moves creating alternative sets of meanings and values, alternative conceptions of what constitutes culture and the relationship between fiction, criticism, politics and power.

In Britain the institutional dominance of liberal-humanist criticism, with its insistence on truth and universality through which it claims to speak for humanity as an ungendered, unclassed, non-racially specific whole, has produced particular strategies of marginalization to deal with alternative critical discourses. The most long-established of these rests on the liberal belief in the impartiality of 'true' education and culture. Within this discursive framework truth transcends political interests and textual readings which look for political implications of whatever kind caricature the truth of the text by their partiality in both senses of the word.

Over recent years the discursive field has taken on a less exclusive and more pluralist aspect. Types of critical discourse incompatible with liberal humanism, for example Marxist, feminist and psychoanalytic criticism may be included in the syllabus of a particular institution but are usually optional. They are not allowed to displace the hegemonic forms of criticism in which the focus is human nature and life itself. Yet the development within the institutions of alternative critical practices has itself been shaped by the discursive power of liberal humanism to dictate what constitutes valid knowledge. Women's writing options within traditional degree schemes or in adult education, for example, have tended to replace the concern with 'human nature' and 'life' found in liberal-humanist criticism with a concentration on women's nature and women's lives. While this can be a valuable, consciousness-raising process for teachers and students, it leaves the male mainstream intact. The current institutional unwillingness in Britain to admit poststructuralism into the mainstream of English studies would seem to suggest that alternative critical practices are acceptable only in so far as they do not challenge the fundamental assumptions of liberal humanism. While it is possible to admit women to 'mankind' and to extend to them the restricted rights of liberalism, it is another thing to challenge humanist conceptions of 'man', 'woman' and the nature of language and power.

The privileging of literature as a special way of acquiring true knowledge about human life and society is not only central to liberal-humanist criticism. It informed much early Marxist criticism such, as the work of Lukács and Goldmann, in which particular theories of the relationship between literature, class and ideology guaranteed the validity of the knowledge of society to be gained from particular types of literature designated 'great'.[1] It is only more recent Marxist criticism in the work of Pierre Macherey (published in France in 1966, but to reach

Britain in English only in 1978) which attempts to theorize the discursive specificity of literary texts and the moves into deconstruction and Foucauldian poststructuralism which have finally offered a thorough-going challenge to those hegemonic forms of humanist criticism which have such deep roots in the development of British critical discourse.

These developments towards a greater diversity in literary criticism have introduced a degree of pluralism into the study of literature which has put into question the fixity of meaning which lies at the heart of liberal-humanist criticism. The way in which most institutions have dealt with this is to hierarchize the significance and value of different readings. This is, however, a constant site of struggle and the plurality of meaning continues to pose a problem for institutions committed to literature as a privileged mode to access to a single truth of human life and nature.

Pluralism relativizes both truth and the social interests which a particular version of truth upholds. Once criticism begins to talk explicitly of social interests, whether of class, race or gender, these issues threaten to transform the terrain of hegemonic liberal forms of criticism. This has made the policing of boundaries particularly important to representatives of the dominant literary discourse. Working-class writing, for example, has been an issue on the margins of literary history, criticism and publishing for at least a hundred years. At moments when the broader political climate was favourable, attention was paid to working-class writing in an attempt to expand or even transform the recognized constitution of the literary field. Acceptable representatives of working-class writing, for example, Walter Greenwood's *Love on the Dole* (1933), were incorporated into the canon by the literary institution. In the process, however, however, they were subject to the politically neutralizing reading strategies of liberal-humanist criticism which sees in them expressions of human nature and fate rather than socially produced political evils.[2] The effect of such readings is to silence the voice of working-class political interests in the text. Women's interests in both female and male authored texts have been similarly consistently silenced by partial critical readings, a point well illustrated by Shoshana Felman in her article on readings of Balzac's *Adieu*, 'Women and Madness: The Critical Phallacy' (Felman, 1975).

At various moments over the last fifty years, for example in the 1930s and at the present moment, some writers, critics and publishing projects have attempted to establish an alternative working-class literary tradition, much as feminists are now attempting to develop traditions of women's writing, black women's writing and lesbian writing.[3] In spite of these attempts, working-class writing has remainded consigned by the dominant discourse and its institutional practices to areas, such as the sociology of literature, which are still marginal within the universities, though less so within polytechnics. More recently it has found a more congenial home in cultural studies, the refuge for all writing which the literary institutions exclude, where it poses little direct challenge to the values that constitute the literary canon.

Gender, Power and the Institution

The hegemony of liberal-humanist literary discourse in Britain long made gender marginal or a non-issue. Liberalism, concerned as it is with unique individuals, is opposed to discourses and political movements which categorize people and privilege social determinations such as gender, race and class over individuality. The political effects of liberal humanism have concerned women writers and critics from the birth of liberalism onwards. Much early feminist political struggle focused on extending to women the basic rights and apparent full subjectivity already possessed by men. Struggle focused on a range of key areas of exclusion such as the law, education and cultural production and this fight continues. In the field of literature it involves the struggle to be heard, to be published and read as woman writer or critic and for women's writing and feminist criticism to be taught within the educational system.

Traditionally the social and educational function of the critic has been not merely to produce 'true' readings but to constitute and maintain certain criteria of literariness. Feminist criticism has attempted to show how these criteria have been implicitly patriarchal, marginalizing gender and rendering women passive recipients of culture rather than its producers, a role compatible with hegemonic norms of femininity outside literary discourse.[4] Many parallels can be drawn between the gender interests represented by the literary institutions and their strategies of inclusion and exclusion. These strategies define what counts as literature, what it is said to mean and who is recognized as an agent either of literary criticism or of literary production.

Marginalization or exclusion, however, have often encouraged oppressed groups to use literature for their own purposes unsanctioned by the institutions. Reading literature is valued by subordinated groups as a way of coming to terms with the experience of oppression, not as something natural but as socially produced. Within the early British labour movement, for example, less well-known working-class writing, as well as socialist classics were a source of alternative ways of understanding working-class oppression and of developing strategies for change.[5] Similarly, literature has long been a powerful source in the sexual–political education of women, offering alternative ways of seeing gender often in relation to class and race and of recognizing forms of patriarchal power. In both cases adult education has been a key site for the practice of politicizing literary education.

Women have been more actively involved in literary production than in many other areas of cultural production. The social relations which in different ways at different historical moments have denied women powerful forms of subjecthood have helped make fiction an important site for the articulation of oppression and of utopian hopes for a different future. The power of fiction lies in its ability to construct for the reader ways of being and of understanding the world. This may involve the illusion of the acquisition of a full subjectivity as in realism or a dissolution of fullness as in post-modernist writing.

Understanding of the exclusion of women from the literary institution, a key focus of feminist critical attention, has become more differentiated in recent years to take account of race, sexual orientation and class. Attempts to contest the marginality both of women in general and of particular groups of women take many forms from the rereading of texts with attention to gender to the recovery, republishing and study of women's writing long since out of print. They involve attention to the positions of women within the institutions which structure the literary field, positions which tend to be less prestigious than those held by men, and efforts to overcome the marginalization of women as professional readers and writers. Attempts to change the literary institution from within are fraught with difficulties and the dangers of compromise or incorporation. For feminists who occupy positions in the literary institutions the contradictions and political choices are always apparent and we need a broader framework than the immediate context within which we work and a long-term view of possible political developments in order to judge best our day-to-day strategies.

Women's writing has long had more of a foothold within the literary institution than other types of marginalized writing. This is due to the existence of 'great' writers, recognized as part of the 'great tradition' who are women. Feminist criticism has not been slow to point out that the texts of Jane Austen, the Brontës, George Eliot and Virginia Woolf have been recognized as 'great', in spite of their female authorship, on the basis of readings which actively repress or marginalize gender concerns within the text. Alternatively, critics have produced readings which reaffirm patriarchal definitions of women. In *The English Novel*, for example, *Jane Eyre* is read as an expression of the author's fundamental concern with

> the pupil–master relationship which is her rationalization, based on her own limited experience of life outside Haworth, of one of the commonest sexual dreams of women: the desire to be mastered, but to be mastered by a man so lofty in his scorn for women as to make the very fact of being mastered a powerful adjunct to the woman's self esteem. (Allen, 1954, p. 179)

Where such readings are not possible critics turn to aesthetic criteria to silence the radical potential of texts by denying them a place in the canon. In the case of Charlotte Brontë's *Shirley*, for example, where tendencies disruptive of the patriarchal status quo are quite explicit in the narrative, the text has been dismissed by some critics as artistically flawed by its concern with the rights of women to self-determination. In the case of Virginia Woolf, where mainstream critics have read her novels as concerned with ultimate truths of a fixed human nature which confirms traditional gender roles, the selection of texts for inclusion in the canon is telling. For example, *Orlando*, the central figure of which changes sex and subject positions as her cultural context alters, elicits far less attention than *Mrs. Dalloway* and is rarely taught. Moreover, Virginia Woolf's explicitly feminist non-fiction texts are held separate from the novels as politically disruptive aberrations. More recent feminist readings of Virginia Woolf's novels have attempted to rescue these texts for feminist interests by stressing their commitment to the dissolution of traditional gender roles and the institution of androgeny.[6]

Feminist Criticism and Women's Writing

The discursive field of feminist criticism is united in its shared political aim of understanding and contesting patriarchal relations. What it means to understand and to contest patriarchy varies from one feminist discourse to another. Differences between discourses result in widely differing forms of political practice. Since its inception, the contemporary Women's Liberation Movement has been an alliance of different forms of feminist practice. The political and theoretical differences between liberal, radical and socialist feminisms outlined in the first chapter of this book have shaped specific areas of feminist analysis, among them cultural and literary criticism. The ways in which liberal, socialist or radical feminism conceptualize gender define their specific political objectives and set the boundaries for the type of question to be asked of any social practice, be it understanding women's work, the family or cultural production.

The development of feminist literary criticism since the late 1960s is marked by often implicit theoretical differences in understanding gender, language and the nature of fictional discourses. It has been shaped both by changes and developments in feminist theory more widely, and by the constraints of the critical discursive field in and against which it has developed. From an early overlap between liberal-humanist feminism and a liberal-humanist critical orthodoxy, in which the feminist project was to contest sexist and misogynist images of women, to allot women writers their rightful place in *the* canon and to constitute a female tradition, the field of feminist critical practice has become much more diverse and radical in its objectives.

From Images of Women to Psychoanalysis and the Discursive Construction of Gender

The initial emphasis in feminist criticism was on analysing the representation of women in fiction and the media as portrayed in texts by both women and men. Some of the most influential texts from the late 1960s and early 1970s are of this kind and include such well-known titles as Kate Millett's *Sexual Politics* (1977), Ellen Moers' *Literary Women* (1978) and Mary Ellmann's *Thinking About Women* (1979). These analyses point to the ways in which women are represented as passive, masochistic and totally male-identified. Relationships with men are shown to dictate the structuring principles of femininity and an un-questioned masculinity lays the boundaries for what women may or may not be. Women are depicted in ways which meet particular forms of male interest and women readers are encouraged to identify with traditional female gender norms of sensibility, passivity and irrationality. Alternatively women are absent from fiction except in so far as they are necessary devices for the depiction of masculinity in texts as, for example, in much popular fiction directed primarily at a male audience, such as thrillers and westerns.

Over the last ten years feminist analysis of the representation of gender in texts has developed from these initial descriptive analyses of images of women to attempts to theorize the ways in which gender is constructed within texts and how representations of gender exercise power over readers. This has meant questioning the nature of language, subjectivity and representation and has involved a move into non-humanist forms of analysis which are predominantly either poststructuralist or psychoanalytic. The most important theoretical shifts have been a rejection, which poststructuralism and psychoanalysis share, of the transparency of language and the unity and fixity of subjectivity. Language is no longer seen as a transparent medium for the expression of meaning ready-constituted in the world beyond language. Masochistic images of femininity, for example, are not reflections of real women any more than the macho heroes of westerns and James Bond novels reflect actual 'real' men. What texts offer are constructions of possible modes of femininity and masculinity together with the forms of psychic and emotional satisfaction and pleasure which these gendered subjectivities bring the individual.

In feminist psychoanalytic criticism critics read texts in the light of Freudian, post-Freudian and Lacanian theories of the acquisition of gendered subjectivity, unconscious processes and the phallocentric structure of the symbolic order. Types of psychoanalytic reading vary but it is to Lacanian theory that most feminist critics look.[7] Their approach involves the assumption that women have no position from which to speak in the symbolic order and that feminine potential is repressed in favour of a patriarchal version of femininity in which male desire and male interests define and control female sexuality and feminine subjecthood. In her book on the cinema, for example, E. Ann Kaplan produces a range of exemplary psychoanalytic readings of films which demonstrate both the strengths and limitations of this approach. She stresses that her concern with psychoanalysis is not with 'necessarily uncovering essential "truth" about the human psyche which exist across historical periods and different cultures', but argues that the cinema is a machine for the 'unconscious release' of the psychic patterns created by capitalist social and interpersonal structures and that psychoanalysis is an appropriate analytic tool for 'understanding and adjusting disturbances caused by the structures which define people':

> To this extent, both mechanisms (film and psychoanalysis) support the status quo; but rather than being necessarily eternal and unchanging in the forms in which we have them, they are inserted in history, linked, that is, to the particular moment of bourgeois capitalism that gave them both their birth.

> If this is so, it is extremely important to use psychoanalysis as a tool, since it will unlock the secrets of our socialization within (capitalist) patriarchy. If we agree that the commercial film (and particularly the genre of melodrama that this book focuses on) took the form it did in some way to satisfy desires and needs created by nineteenth-century familial organization (an organization that produces Oedipal traumas), then psychoanalysis becomes a crucial tool for explaining the needs, desires and male-female positionings that are reflected in film. The signs in the Hollywood film convey the patriarchal ideology that underlies our social structures and that constructs women in very specific ways – ways that reflect patriarchal needs, the patriarchal unconscious. (Kaplan, 1983, p. 24)

The readings which follow are coherent, convincing accounts of the meaning of the films in terms of psychoanalytic concepts, but as Kaplan herself acknowledges, they rely on an acceptance of the terms of psychoanalysis and the privileging of this account of the acquisition of gender difference, and of sexuality in this process. There are problems with assuming the effectivity within texts of psychoanalytic structures of gender identity which have a material basis in anatomical difference which guarantees the subordination of women to men, and with looking for their exemplification in filmic or literary texts. In this approach, meaning is reduced to a particular version of sexuality and gender, and changes are limited to a revolution in the psycho-sexual structures which are thought currently to structure gender identity, power and the symbolic order. Even if the universal psycho-sexual relations of Freud and Lacan are seen as historically specific to Western capitalist patriarchy, it is not clear how fundamental changes in the processes of psycho-sexual development could be achieved, given the lack of women's access to signification, the all-defining nature of the symbolic order and the interests which it serves which are capitalist, racist and patriarchal.

We need to ask whether or not it is necessary to assume the appropriateness to capitalist patriarchy of Freud's account of psycho-sexual development in order to interpet aspects of the symbolic order. Can we not ask questions of the representation of women, women's subjectivity, our access to language, the constitution of modes of pleasure, the marginality and centrality of particular forms of discourse and the power and interests which they represent or suppress without linking readings to a fixed Freudian model of psycho-sexual development? It is possible to start from the range of existing discourses which constitute the symbolic order, of which psychoanlysis is but one, and to look in a differentiated way at their structure and implications for desire, femininity and masculinity and their social power and effectivity. If we take this approach, the unconscious is not limited to psycho-sexual organization. It encompasses much more than the organization of sexual difference.

In Lacanian-based psychoanalytic criticism historically pro-duced language constructs rather than reflects meaning but it constructs meaning according to particular pre-given structures of meaning, defined in relation to the primary signifier of sexual difference, the phallus, and the unconscious structures which found the patriarchal order. In feminist poststructuralism, however, there can be no ultimate fixing of femininity, masculinity or unconscious structures. They are always historically produced through a range of discursive practices much wider than those of the immediate nuclear family and both the symbolic order and the unconscious are marked by difference, contradiction and pressures for conservation or for change.

The parallel questioning of subjectivity which has been an

important factor in recent feminist work on representation, has focused on decentring the unitary self-present subject of humanist discourse. Once again this move is shared by both poststructuralism and psychoanalysis. Yet whereas for psychoanalysis subjectivity is precarious only within the terms of the psycho-sexual structures of the individual, where consciousness is in conflict with the unconscious, feminist poststructuralism sees subjectivity as the site of conflicting and competing subject positions. In constructing meanings for us, language, in the form of a multitude of different discourses, constructs different possible modes of subjectivity. Conflict comes from the attempt to take up a single, unified position in competing or incoherent discourses. These subject positions constitute desire in particular ways and imply particular forms of repression. Thus feminist poststructuralism does not deny unconscious processes, for example, the attempt to reconcile the irreconcilable may lead to hysteria, but locates the conflict involved in the symbolic order, not in psycho-sexual structures.

These theoretical developments within feminist criticism have given rise to analyses of wide-ranging cultural products and practices, for example, Rosalind Coward's *Female Desire*, a very accessible poststructuralist book which draws at times on psychoanalysis. *Female Desire* works from the assumption that gendered subjectivity is discursively constructed within signifying practices and analyses the ways in which a range of cultural phenomena construct women's pleasure 'from food to family snapshots, from royalty to nature programmes' (Coward, 1984, p.13). It resists any conception of an essential repressed or distorted female pleasure, seeing female pleasures and the modes of femininity which they constitute as produced by cultural practices: 'Feminine positions are produced as responses to the pleasures offered to us; our subjectivity and identity are formed in the definitions of desire which encircle us. These are the experiences which make change such a difficult and daunting task, for female desire is constantly lured by discourses which sustain male privilege' (p. 16). Rosalind Coward points to how 'female dissatisfaction is constantly recast as desire', most often desires which commodities such as clothes, make-up, furnishings or cordon blue cooking promise to fulfil. But while these are the most visible cultural constructions of female desire and femininity, they are not the whole story. Women get pleasure from things which do not reinforce patriarchal society. Moreover cultural constructions of female desire are constantly being challenged and can be changed.

Most of the poststructuralist cultural criticism which British feminists have produced until now has been in the area of popular culture and visual representation. Analysis of the cinema and even feminist film making, for example, are strong sites of this work. As yet it has made only a small impact on literary studies. This can be understood in part as the result of particular historical conditions. Work on the media and popular culture developed rapidly at the moment when psychoanalytic and poststructuralist theories first began to make an impact in Britain. It was a relatively new areas of study, open to definition. Literary studies, on the other hand, were firmly ensconced within the cultural and educational institutions as a liberal-humanist discipline profoundly hostile to new theoretical innovations which questioned the truth of its own practices. It has taken years to begin to challenge effectively the naturalness of liberal-humanist modes of reading.

Fiction as an Expression of Women's Experience

Whereas recent work on representation has looked at the mechanisms through which meaning is constructed for the reader and how fictive articulations of gender relate to the wider discursive fields of gender relations, the other influential branch of feminist criticism looks to fiction as an expression of already constituted gendered experience.[8] Starting from the traditional literary canon, feminist critics have noted the absence from most canonical texts of a female perspective and a 'true to life' representation of women's experience. The most common explanation of this absence offered by feminist critics is the masculine gender of most authors, whose work is seen to reflect a male experience. This is reflected both in representations of women in texts and in the absence from many canonical texts of detailed treatment of the' spheres in which women have traditionally been active and have had a voice, above all the sphere of domesticity. It is to women's writing and particularly to women's depiction of this sphere that these critics turn.

Domesticity and personal relations have long been a key theme of women's fiction. From women's writing of the eighteenth century to the most recent novels by avowedly feminist writers such as Lisa Alther and Marge Piercy, the concern is more often with sexual and family relationships than with areas which are thought to constitute public life. This sexual division within fiction can be understood in terms of the wider sexual division of labour and powerful norms of femininity and masculinity which have circumscribed women's and men's access to particular areas of life and the discourses of gender, work and domesticity which structure them. Yet it can also be seen as an effect of the direct ways in which men wield power over women in family and sexual relationships.

The study of women's writing as a feminist project can take many forms depending on the assumptions and perspectives of the reader. It is possible, for example, to look at it in both essentialist and poststructuralist ways and the key difference in these approaches is the significance given to women as authors. Essentialist approaches assume that female authorship of texts is their most crucial aspect and that they are the product of a specifically female experience and aesthetic. In poststructuralist theory authorship does not guarantee meaning, though the historical context in which the author is located will produce the discourses of the text. The forms of gendered subjectivity offered by texts are also the product of the social discourses on gender in circulation at the time of writing.

Up to now the dominant concern of most feminist critics of women's writing has been with identifying women's experience and an authentic female voice in these texts, a concern which places their work within the essentialist camp. Ultimately their critical texts seek out an essence of femininity which makes women's writing qualitatively different from writing by men and this quality is located in a female, black or lesbian aesthetic and more specifically in women's language. It is assumed that a female aesthetic will be found in the text, but it is the author who guarantees the presence of this difference by her womanhood. The reasons for the gender differences which the texts express are variously assumed to be biologically, psycho-sexually or historically produced. Most often, however, they are seen as the effect on women writers of the patriarchal society in which they live, a society which denies women any position from which to express directly an authentic female voice.

The privileging of female authorship and the aim of identifying a female language and aesthetic has come to be known as woman-centred criticism. This form of criticism has produced texts which are now widely regarded as feminist classics, in particular Elaine Showalter's *A Literature of Their Own* (1977) and Sandra Gilbert and Susan Gubar's study of nineteenth-century women's writing, *The Mad Woman in the Attic* (1979). In these texts the critics are concerned with reading women's writing as an effect of and challenge to patriarchy. In a broad literary history Elaine Showalter traces a shift from writing imitative of male-authored texts through feminist challenges to women-centred writing which, she says, has been the dominant mode since the 1920s. Gilbert and Gubar's project is more specific. They look to the ways in which writing is defined as a male activity and the effect of this on women's attempts to articulate a distinctive female voice.

Gilbert and Gubar stress the similarities between women writers, assuming an identity between author and text or author and particular characters. For example, they identify madness as a form of resistance to patriarchy through which an authentic female voice can assert itself. *The Mad Woman in the Attic* shows how writers in nineteenth-century patriarchal society are positioned as women by dominant discourses of femininity which polarize it into dualities like the angel in the house and the monster woman. In doing so they make important points about the continuities in patriarchal discourse but risk making patriarchy seem like a seamless web against which the repressed authentic female voice is powerless. The problem is lack of specificity in analysing both the changing structures and practices in which patriarchal power is exercised and the changing modes of femininity which become possible at particular historical moments. Rather than patriarchy as a fixed structure and femaleness and the female voice as a response to this structure we need to look at the web of modes of patriarchal power and the range of feminine voices and subject positions which support and resist them.

Woman-centred criticism which focuses on the recovery and re-evaluation of women's writing as an expression of women's experience has been given the name *gynocritics* by the influential American feminist critic Elaine Showalter. Writing in *Women Writing and Writing about Women* (Jacobus, 1979), Showalter defined the project of gynocritics as:

> to construct a female framework for the analysis of women's literature, to develop new models based on the study of female experience, rather than to adopt male models and theories. Gynocritics begins at the point when we free ourselves from the linear absolutes of male literary history, stop trying to fit women between the lines of the male tradition, and focus instead on the newly visible world of female culture. (p. 28)

More recently in 'Feminist Criticism in the Wilderness' (1985), she defines male critical theory as 'a concept of creativity, literary history or literary interpretation based entirely on male experience and put forward as universal' (Showalter, 1985, p. 247). The development of woman-centred criticism has given rise to 'the study of women *as writers*, and its subjects are the history, styles, themes, genres and structures of writing by women; the psychodynamics of female creativity; the trajectory of the individual or collective female career; the evolution and laws of a female literary tradition' (p. 248)

The 'history, styles, themes, genres and structures of writing by women' can be studied in various ways depending on the political objectives of the feminist critic. From a poststructuralist perspective, for example, these aspects of writing contribute to an understanding of the range of discourses of gender in circulation and the subject positions available to women both at particular moments in history and in the present. Looked at in their historical specificity they demonstrate what it was possible for women to say about the patriarchal societies within which they lived from a specific discursive context, that of fiction, and how it was possible to say things. This in turn gives insight into the specific structures of patriarchal power and the possibilities of resistance to it.

In Elaine Showalter's formulation, the project is different. It is to uncover 'the evolution and laws of a female literary tradition'. The assumption that it is possible to construct the history and laws of a single female tradition suggests that there is something quite specific to women's writing and female creativity which transcends its immediate historical context. It has essential qualities. In works of criticism written in this mode, these qualities are identified in the use of language and textual strategies employed by women writers. Sandra Gilbert and Susan Gubar, for instance, point to the recurrence of themes and images found in nineteenth-century women's writing and look for evidence of a female voice, while in *A Literature of Their Own*, Elaine Showalter looks for the expression of authentic women's experience.

Feminist poststructuralism suggests that the textual strategies employed in women's writing are determined by the constraints and possibilities of the class- and racially specific patriarchal societies within which writers and their access to aesthetic discourse are located. Only wider detailed discursive analysis of the period can show the extent to which they are specific to women and why this should be the case. Broader analysis will also throw light on how texts resist and transcend accepted gender definitions. This is the case for all types of women's writing, so, for example, as Deborah McDowell points out in her article on black feminist criticism (Showalter, 1985, pp. 186–99), it is necessary to look at black women's writing in the context of black male writing as well as in its difference from white writing in order to produce a specifically black female aesthetic.

There is perhaps a more fundamental question which needs to be asked of feminist criticism dedicated to constructing traditions.

This is how the project of producing laws of a female literary tradition, black or white, lesbian or heterosexual, is politically useful to feminism. Certainly it is politically comforting to know that other women have had difficulty in coming to terms with or accepting their gender definition under patriarchy and to realize that neither gender nor the specific forms taken by patriarchy are static. This is also the case where racial and class oppression are concerned. However, the danger in formulating general laws about women's writing is that they render differences and contradictions invisible, differences which are at least as important as similarities and which tell us more about the precise discursive structuring of gender at any particular historical moment. Moreover, general laws inevitably set limits to femininity and implicitly prescribe the effectivity of women's fiction and the possibilities of historical change. In practice we look to women's writing for many different things. It may be for positive role models, for example, images of strong and resistant black women or lesbians, or for imaginative alternatives to existing patriarchal society as in some feminist utopian and science fiction. In all cases, however, the questions we ask are shaped by the concerns of their moment of articulation and these concerns are constantly in the process of redefinition.

This does not mean that it is unproductive to study women's writing in isolation from male-authored texts. The close connection between the social location of women and the themes of their writing which have led much recent feminist criticism to turn exclusively to women's writing as a field of study are crucial to our understanding of patriarchy. The socially and historically produced concerns of women writers as depicted in fiction help to form a map of the possible subject positions open to women, what they could say or not from within the discursive field of femininity in which they were located. In the nineteenth century, many women writers opted to speak out through male pseudonyms and their texts point to the impossibility of finally resolving women's aspirations to independence and self-determination within the social and legal relations of the day. Legally and financially independent heroines such as Jane Eyre and Shirley Keeldar are relocated in families as financially dependent wives who are their husband's property in often unconvincing or unsatisfying narrative closures.

The political point to be made here is that it is perhaps more helpful to the feminist cause to look for difference and contradictions in the ways in which women's writing addresses patriarchal power relations and in the subject positions which it offers its readers. This is particularly the case if we are interested in transforming existing modes of gendered subjectivity. The impetus to produce a general theory of female creativity for the present from the work of writers who are the product of different societies and historical moments in which patriarchal power was exercised in quite specific and changing discursive practices has to be understood in the context of current concerns within the Women's Liberation Movement with identifying and developing a specifically female culture. This aim, which has all the powerful attraction of separatist politics, ultimately relies on an essential femaleness which is actually quite historically and socially specific. The question we must ask is whether this femaleness is what we want and whether it offers a useful point of political challenge and resistance to patriarchal discourses and gendered subject positions.

Similar questions need to be asked of feminist criticism which is concerned with discovering particular women's experience in women's writing. At the present time attempts are being made to describe black and lesbian female experience as expressed in women's writing and to construct traditions of black and lesbian women's writing. As with all traditions, readers assume that texts are connected, that earlier writers influence later ones and that the analysis of such influences comes before the detailed historical location of women's writing within the specific social relations of cultural production, structured by class, gender and race, which produce texts.

The problems facing this approach are at their most extreme in the case of lesbian writing and the construction of a lesbian aesthetic and tradition expressing a lesbian experience. Not only does this project share the problems of approaches which assume that texts express women's experience, it is also faced with the primary problem of defining lesbian texts. In her overview of lesbian-feminist literary criticism, written in 1981, Bonnie Zimmerman addresses the complexities of these issues. She points out that contemporary discourses of lesbianism are wide-ranging. They include the exclusive definition of lesbianism as a sexual practice, the extension of the term lesbian to all 'woman-identified experience' as in the work of Adrienne Rich, or some point between the two. Zimmerman herself endorses Lillian Faderman's definition in *Surpassing the Love of Men* (Faderman, 1981):

> 'Lesbian' describes a relationship in which two women's strongest emotions and affections are directed toward each other. Sexual contact may be part of the relationship to a greater or lesser degree, or it may be entirely absent. By preference the two women spend most of their time together and share most aspects of their lives . . . with each other. (Faderman in Showalter, 1985, p. 206)

This definition may indeed serve the interests of current lesbian research and attempts to construct a lesbian tradition. It is important to remember, however, that it is a contemporary definition and that the meaning of lesbianism changes with historical shifts in the discursive construction of female sexuality. The different meanings of lesbianism in the past gave rise to different forms of oppression and resistance, knowledge of which helps to denaturalize the present and sharpen our awareness of the contemporary modes through which gender and sexual power are exercised.

As a group who are socially defined by others in terms of a sexual preference which is not heterosexual and therefore not 'normal', lesbians write from different subject positions than most heterosexual feminists. It is not impossible for heterosexual women to occupy fundamentally- anti-heterosexist discourses but this takes a political commitment beyond their own immediate day-to-day interests. While all feminists would agree 'that a woman's identity is not defined only by her relation to a male world and a male literary tradition . . . that powerful bonds between women are a crucial factor in women's lives' (Showalter,

1985, p. 201), this is not enough to counter a heterosexism which is a fundamental structuring principle of discourses of gender and the social practices which they imply.

If it is difficult to decide on the meaning of lesbianism in women, a decision which can only ultimately be political, determined by present and future objectives, the question of what constitutes a lesbian text is equally open to a range of answers: 'This critic will need to consider whether a lesbian text is one written by a lesbian (and if so, how do we determine who is a lesbian?), one written about lesbians (which might be by a heterosexual woman or man), or one that expresses a lesbian 'vision' (which has to be satisfactorily outlined) (Zimmerman in Showalter, 1985, p. 208).

The questions asked by self-defined lesbian critics tend to focus on the relationship between author and text. Zimmerman, for example, assumes that 'the sexual and emotional orientation of a woman profoundly affects her consciousness and thus her creativity' (Showalter, 1985, p. 201). While this is very likely to be the case, we cannot know the intimate details of an author's consciousness; at best we have access to the competing range of subject positions open to her at a particular historical moment. Moreover we cannot look to authorial consciousness for the meaning of a text, since this is always open to plural readings which are themselves the product of specific discursive contexts.

Alternatively lesbianism in fiction can be seen in terms of textual strategies as, for example, in Barbara Smith's exposition of Toni Morrison's *Sula* in the same volume of essays (Showalter, 1985, pp. 168–84). There is a danger, however, of masking important and productive differences by assuming that fiction which contests particular forms of heterosexual practice and family life is necessarily lesbian in its implications.

How we define lesbianism and how we read lesbian texts will depend on how we define our objectives. Bonnie Zimmerman opts for a 'lesbian "essence" that may be located in all these specific historical existences, just as we may speak of a widespread perhaps universal structure of marriage or the family' (Showalter, 1985, pp. 215–16). She stresses, however, that 'differences are as significant as similarities'. If we are searching for positive lesbian role models or for a recognizable lesbian aesthetic, then a fixed concept of lesbianism is important. From a poststructuralist perspective, however, this fixing is always historically specific and temporary and will determine in advance the type of answers we get to our questions. If we want to understand and challenge past and present heterosexism we need to start from the discourses which constitute it and the forms of sexuality, sexual regulation and gendered subjectivity which they construct. We need to look for the possibilities of challenge and resistance to specific modes of heterosexuality. Fictional texts play their part in this process.

Black feminist criticism shares some of the problems faced by lesbian feminist criticism. While there is little debate about whether a text is a black text or a text of colour, this is guaranteed by the author, problems arise over identifying authentic black experience in black women's writing and in constituting an 'identifiable literary tradition' (Barbara Smith in Showalter, 1985, p. 174). Critics can start from the assumption that 'thematically, stylistically, aesthetically and conceptually Black women writers manifest common approaches to the art of creating literature as a direct result of the specific political, social and economic experience they have been obliged to share' (Showalter, 1985, p. 174). Alternatively we can look at black women's writing in its historically produced specificity, at-tempting to account for the discourses and social practices which have produced individual texts and which may well give rise to similarities between writers but also to differences. The critic of black feminist writing may choose to use existing critical tools, for example, poststructuralism, or as Barbara Smith recommends, reject them and 'write out of her own identity' in an explicitly humanist approach to black consciousness and subjec-tivity which implicitly restricts white access to black women's writing (p. 175). As with lesbian criticism, the methodology best used by critics of black women's writing is a question of politics. How we read black fiction will determine what insight we can gain from it into the discursive strategies of sexism and racism. As Susan Willis argues in her critical perspective on Black women's writing 'Black women's writing is not a mere collection of motifs and strategies, but a mode of discourse which enables a critical perspective upon the past, the present and sometimes into an emerging future' (Greene and Kahn, 1985, p. 220).

The concept of authorship which guarantees most feminist readings of black, white and lesbian women's writing is shared with liberal-humanist criticism. The author is the speaking, full, self-present subject producing the text from her own knowledge of the world and she is the guarantee of its truth. The effect of this discourse is to fix meaning. Traditionally author-centred criticism seeks to get inside the artist's mind and interpret what she/he really meant for the benefit of the ordinary reader. At its best this critical method involves close textual reading and the detailed knowledge of biography and non-literary writing, such as letters and diaries. From this material attempts are made to reconstruct the creative process through the exploration of textual influences and differences in the various versions of any particular piece of writing. It assumes that artistic intention is what is important and is the source and guarantee of the meaning of a text. It is a project which is fundamentally flawed by the impossibility of ever knowing what an author intended. Moreover authorial intention, even when apparently voiced in aesthetic theory, is no guarantee of the meaning of the actual fictional text. In the case of feminist author-based criticism it is the writer's biological and social femaleness which guarantees its gender perspectives. Similarly in black feminist criticism the race, gender and class of the writer is the guarantee of the meaning and authenticity of the text.[9]

From a feminist poststructuralist perspective authorship cannot be the source of the authority of meaning any more than the individual speaking subject, the agent of discourse, is its origin. This is not, however, to say that there is no place in feminist criticism for a study of authors, provided that critics recognize that accounts of authors are themselves discursive constructs and not a key to meaning.

The humanist concern with authorship creates the space for issues of class, race and gender but in ways that attempt to fix the meaning of texts once and for all, irrespective of the reader or the reading context. While the biography of authors is of interest to feminists and may help to explain the social and institutional location of women writers and the formal techniques which they employ, it cannot be taken as the guarantee of the meaning of a text. To read a text in the light of the biography of the author, which is itself a discursive construct, which can be more or less enlightening depending on how it is constructed, is but one way of reading. In choosing a mode of reading we need to ask what useful political questions it answers. To be politically effective a reading needs to address the ideological and political concerns of the present-day reader.

It is possible to abandon the liberal-humanist preoccupation with authorship and shift the emphasis onto the text itself without producing readings which necessarily threaten the terrain of hegemonic criticism with its insistence on the non-political nature of great literature. This is very much what 'new criticism' and, more recently, some forms of deconstruction have done. New criticism, which is now an established mode of critical practice, rejects authorship as the guarantee of meaning arguing that authorial intentions are inaccessible and authorial statements of intent cannot be taken at face value. Nor is meaning to be found in the reader's response, it is a function of the text. This meaning remains, however, unitary and universal. It is this assumption of the presence of a single, true meaning in the text which deconstruction and other forms of poststructuralism question.[10]

Forms of Poststructuralist Criticism

Deconstruction as a critical practice is based on the work of Jacques Derrida. It arises out of a fundamental critique of humanist discourses and their conceptions of subjectivity and language. It rejects unitary intentional subjectivity, locating meaning in texts and their relation with other texts, insisting that this meaning is not only plural but constantly deferred in the never-ending webs of textuality in which all texts are located. Derrida argues that all criticism is predicated on specific

philosophical precepts. These are necessarily hierarchial oppositions, such as man/woman or culture/nature, which, in keeping
with the structures of logocentrism, make one side of the
opposition the key concept in relation to which the other is
defined negatively. Deconstruction, by reversing these oppositions, is able to show how discourses achieve their effects,
rhetorically, and to displace their systems. This constitutes an
intervention in the field of oppositions which, Derrida argues, is
also a field of non-discursive forces.

All criticism is necessarily implicated in logocentrism, the
fixing of meanings through the assumption of privileged key
premises, and the critic, far from being able to escape this
process, should be actively aware of the implications of a
discourse. It is the metaphysics of presence which makes
consciousness, for example, the mind of the speaker or writer,
the source and guarantee of meaning. In deconstruction,
meaning is deferred in the differential relations between all other
meanings inscribed in the structure of language, the traces of
which affect the meaning in question. These meanings inhere in
what Derrida calls an *archi-écriture* or proto-writing, which is
the precondition for speech or writing. 'Différance', differing
and deferral, are both a condition of signification and a
signifying act which takes place in a specific context. As
Jonathan Culler argues in *On Deconstruction*, meaning is always
an historical product, produced 'in processes of contextualization, decontexualization and recontextualization', but history
cannot fix meaning by being its foundation:

> Derrida uses history against philosophy: when confronted
> with essentialist, idealizing theories and claims to ahistorical
> or transhistorical understanding, he asserts the historicity
> of these discourses and theoretical assumptions. But he also
> uses philosophy against history and the claims of historical
> narratives. Deconstruction couples a philosophical critique
> of history and historical understanding with the specifi-
> cation that discourse is historical and meaning historically
> determined, both in principle and in practice . . .

As should now be clear, deconstruction is not a theory that defines meaning in order to tell you how to find it. As a critical undoing of the hierarchical oppositions on which theories depend, it demonstrates the difficulty of any theory that would define meaning in a univocal way: as what an author intends, what conventions determine, what a reader experiences. (Culler, 1983, pp. 129–31)

Deconstruction is useful for feminism in so far as it offers a method of decentring the hierarchical oppositions which underpin gender, race and class oppression and of instigating new, more progressive theories. Gayatri Spivak, for example, has used deconstruction in the interests of a progressive politics of gender and race (1985). However, much deconstructive analysis, especially in American literary criticism, fails to attend to questions of social context, particular interests and power. While its stress on the plurality and non-fixity of meaning is a helpful move beyond criticism which attempts to identify one true meaning, the implicit assumption that there is a free play of meaning not already located in a hierarchical network of discursive relations is to deny social power by rendering it invisible and therefore to reaffirm the status quo. Deconstructionist approaches to textual analysis which share a disregard for the wider historically specific discursive context of reading and writing and the power relations which structure the literary field itself do not meet feminist needs. The interests which inform deconstructionist criticism as a purely textual criticism are generally the unacknowledged interests of individual readers, most often those supporting white middle-class patriarchy.

The recent developments in feminist criticism in France, discussed in chapter 3, have seen the replacement of the female or male author as guarantee of meaning by a theory of textuality in which writing strategies are said to be either feminine or masculine, disruptive or conservative. Influenced by both psychoanalytic and deconstructionist approaches to subjectivity and language, this criticism tends towards general theories of the feminine, female sexuality and language which do not take account of historical difference. Where, as in the work of Julia

Kristeva, femininity is defined as property of language it either becomes divorced from the historically produced feminine subjectivities which women inhabit or severely circumscribes the possibility of resistant femininity, identifying them with the marginalized, silenced and repressed aspects of a monolithically patriarchal symbolic order. Where femininity/femaleness is located in a particular discourse of female sexuality as in the work of Luce Irigaray, women are offered modes of subjectivity beyond the symbolic order which challenge fixity and unitariness but fail to address the specific discursive modes through which patriarchal power is exercised, offering a form of anti-rational separatist plural subjectivity founded on female sexuality. Hélène Cixous's work aims to theorize feminine writing rather than subjectivity in terms of female libido and language which patriarchy represses and which returns in feminine writing to threaten and undermine the phallocentric and logocentric order. Like Irigaray, she locates the feminine libido which gives rise to feminine writing under patriarchy in women and in particular in their sexuality.

To remain at the level of textual analysis, irrespective of the discursive context and the power/knowledge relations of the discursive field within which textual readings are located cannot be sufficient for feminist practice. Nor can it be enough to see these power/knowledge relations in terms of a general all-encompassing theory of patriarchy in which resistance is confined to the extra-symbolic. While discourses of female sexuality and femininity are key structuring principles of the patriarchal order, they are not static nor can all forms of patriarchal power be reduce to sexuality or sexual analogy. In literary and cultural criticism it is ultimately reductive to read texts only for the feminine challenge of their language or for an authentic female voice. While such reduction is often a valid and important political strategy, we should never lose sight of the broader field of struggle in which not just femininity but gender, class and race are key political concerns. It is only by redrawing the map of the literary discursive field and redefining the discipline that the place of literature in the wider field of power/knowledge relations can be made clear.

For poststructuralist feminism literature is one specific site among many where the ideological construction of gender takes place. Rather than reflecting or expressing socially produced or essential womanhood, literature, like other forms of discourse, is concerned to construct apparently 'natural' ways of being a woman or man. Fictional texts offer their readers subject positions and modes of subjectivity which imply particular meanings, values and forms of pleasure. Central to the views of society offered by a text are particular definitions of femininity and its relation to masculinity.

Feminist poststructuralist insistence on the autonomy of the meaning of texts as regards authorship and on texts as constructions rather than reflections of meaning implies a necessary change of perspective and emphasis for feminist criticism. The central focus of interest becomes the way in which texts construct meanings and subject positions for the reader, the contradictions inherent in this process and its political implications, both in its historical context and in the present.

Feminist poststructuralist approaches deny the central humanist assumption that women or men have essential natures. They insist on the social construction of gender in discourse, a social construction which encompasses desire, the unconscious and conscious emotional life. Feminist poststructuralism refuses to fall back on general theories of the feminine psyche or biologically based definitions of femininity which locate its essence in processes such as motherhood or female sexuality. There can be no guarantee of the nature of women's experience since, in so far as it is meaningful, this experience is discursively produced by the constitution of women as subjects within historically and socially specific discourses. This does not rule out the specificity of women's experiences and their difference from those of men, since, under patriarchy, women have differential access to the discursive field which constitutes gender, gendered experience and gender relations of power in society. However, women's subjectivity will always be open to the plurality of meaning and the possibilities contained within this plurality will have different political implications.

While the gender, race, sexual orientation or class of authors do not guarantee the meaning of fictive representations in their texts, male-authored texts are likely to have a greater investment in traditional gender norms. The social construction of masculine subjectivities tends to serve patriarchal interests which allot more power to men. However, women, too, are governed as subjects by patriarchal norms and values. Given the social location of women both as women and as writers and the modes of femininity available to them at any historical moment, women's writing may well be more ideologically fractured and more open to oppositional readings than texts by male authors of the same period, but this is something which requires demonstration and cannot be assumed. Similarly, the race and ethnic background of a writer does not guarantee the race politics of a text. The task for feminist criticism is to demonstrate how texts constitute gender for the reader in class-and race-specific ways and how these modes of femininity and masculinity relate to the broader network of discourses on gender both in the past and in the present. Poststructuralist feminist analysis is involved in the discursive battle for the meaning of texts which is a constant feature of the literary and educational institutions, as well as the everyday practice of reading. It is a battle in which the legitimation of particular readings and the exclusion of others represent quite specific patriarchal, class and race interests, helping to constitute our common-sense assumptions as reading and speaking subjects.

Strategies for Change

If feminist poststructuralism offers a way of analysing the power/knowledge relations which structure the literary discursive field and of placing literary discourse within the broader discursive framework of contemporary society, feminism insists that we work to change these power/knowledge relations. Since power is exercised through the constitution of subjectivity within discourse and the production of social agents, it is important to understand the hierarchical network and the contradictions and weak points in the discursive field.

In order to contest the marginalization of feminist interests we need to ask how the literary institutions, where texts, modes of reading, meanings and values are legitimated, maintain the hegemonic structure of the discursive field. We must analyse what power/knowledge relations constitute this field, how power is exercised, whose interests are silenced, marginalized or excluded and how open it is to change.

At the heart of the mechanisms of power/knowledge lies the education system, within which selected individuals are initiated into literary discourse, taught to read in particular ways and to specific ends. The location of literary studies as an area separate from literacy and the broader processes of selection and exclusion within education ensure that only a minority of children are subjected to the full impact of a literary education. This education is geared towards the requirements of the public examinations which are informed by the assumptions, values and modes of criticism preferred within the universities. Thus, school students at both GCSE and A-level are encouraged to analyse characters as if they were real but ungendered indi-viduals, to treat texts as if they were expressions of real life and to look for universal human values within the standard range of classics and modern texts which compose the syllabuses.[11]

A literary education involves learning to read but also to speak or write. In the reading process the reader is subject to the textual strategies of the writing in question and its attempts to position her as subject and extend to her its values and view of the world. To deny these strategies is to refuse to read the text in question, though as Pierre Macherey has demonstrated, all texts contain inconsistencies, contradictions and silences, moments when the limits of the discourses which constitute the text become visible and the project of the text is shown to be partial in the sense of speaking for particular non-totalizing interests.[12] The practice of criticism involves taking up a position on the meaning of a text and fixing it through the production of a reading. This process requires the individual to occupy the position of speaking subject within a specific critical discourse with all the assumptions that this implies.

Ways of reading are produced within discourse. In order to be effective, discourses need to be in circulation, available to people, providing possible modes of subjectivity. Which texts are available, which remain in print, which are widely disseminated through education and publishing is not a neutral issue. It is possible to trace the formative power of patriarchal, class and racial interests not just in modes of reading and the constitution of the canon, but in what is available to be read at all. In the case of much widely available fiction, it is possible to determine a convergence of capitalist interests in profit and broader hegemonic interests in the reproduction of the relations of production and reproduction in class, gender and racial terms. Two obvious examples of this are pornography and romance. The one is marketed for men, the other for women. Both deal with the nature of gender and gender difference. Both constitute gendered forms of subjectivity for the reader in ways that leave existing gender norms and the sexual division of labour intact. Alternatively, the suppression through silencing of texts which bear witness to resistance among women to their patriarchal definition over the last 300 years has also played its part in reaffirming the patriarchal status quo by depriving women of the knowledge of the history of alternative resistant subject positions which make clear the non-natural status of current gender norms.

The recent moves to reclaim and reprint women's writing and to publish new writing by women are important because they make available previously unavailable texts. Yet as many of the reprinted women's novels show, being a woman is no guarantee that one's writing will challenge hegemonic norms or employ a different, resistant and specifically female discourse. Much women's writing, not least of all romance, reproduces forms of discourse which place women firmly within patriarchal relations and encourage them to identify themselves with masochistic forms of femininity and to find pleasure in doing so. They offer women modes of femininity and of female desire which deny their own social construction, proclaiming themselves to be natural. Challenge to accepted gender norms requires new ways of understanding gender as historically produced and changeable. It is here that feminist theory is so important.

Most women's writing and all popular fiction do not come

within the bounds of 'literature'. They are not legitimated by the literary institutions and are not seen as modes of access to the truth about 'human nature'. However, the fact that they are not defined as 'literature' does not detract from their discursive power to transmit meanings and values. This process continues both in spite of and because of the practice of recognized literary, educational and cultural institutions. Girls are taught basic skills in reading which involve reading in particular ways to specific ends. Most are then left to the attractions of the market place. This includes magazines as well as fiction in novel form. Popular fiction, read as it most often is for pleasure, works on these basic skills and extends and confirms the expectations of the reading subject. It is arguable that the absence of popular fiction from most literary critical discourses of reading helps popular fiction to shape the reader's sense of pleasure more directly and leaves it open to more powerful, apparently 'natural' modes of reading. As with literature its power and effectivity lie in the role it plays in the battle for subjects, helping to constitute them in conservative, chauvinist or in the case of some feminist fiction, radical ways. The institutional marginalization of popular fiction helps to further the myth that it is pure entertainment, a condition conducive to its ideological work.

Fiction has long been seen as a powerful form of education in social meanings and values, as an effective purveyor of beliefs about gender, race and class. Yet if it is this, then it is also a powerful resource for those interests which to date had been marginalized, excluded or silenced by the dominant culture. The effectivity of fiction lies in the reading process itself. In this process the reader is offered subjectivity, subjected to the organizing principle, meanings and values which it is the text's project to establish. Textual strategies vary but most common, both in popular and other fiction are the strategies of narrative, characterization and confession.

The tension within the Women's Liberation Movement between humanist forms of feminism, which seek to affirm true forms of femininity, and psychoanalytic and poststructuralist forms, in which femininity is a psycho-sexual or social construct, extends to the realm of fiction. Humanist feminists have tended to be drawn to realist fiction, constructing their general theories of women's writing, women's language and feminist aesthetics accordingly. In doing so they have rejected texts which contest the apparent transparency and closure of meaning in realism and attempt to deconstruct the fixity of meaning. In theoretical terms this has produced oppositions in which, on the one hand, realism is viewed as the most appropriate mode for expressing women's authentic experience while at the other extreme, in French theories of feminine writing, it is aligned with the patriarchal symbolic order. Both positions fail to take account of the historical and social specificity of reading and writing, creating an opposition which narrows the possibilities for radically political feminist ways of reading and writing.

It is as limiting to reject all non-realist writing as it is to reduce realist techniques to phallocentrism or to place the feminine completely outside the symbolic order of rationality. We need to look at fictional form as an historically produced discursive construct effective in different ways in different contexts. In choosing between fictional forms, as between modes of reading, we need to define political objectives and interests and work accordingly, always aware of the implications of the questions and forms of closure in operation and their social and historical specificity. There is a place both for realism and for deconstructive writing. Women need access to the different subject positions offered in imaginative alternatives to the present, in humorous critiques and even by positive heroines. While we need texts that affirm marginalized subject positions, however, it is important to be constantly wary of the dangers of fixing subject positions and meanings beyond the moment when they are politically productive. We also need ways of reading which see texts for what they are – partisan discursive constructs offering particular meanings and modes of understanding.

Feminist poststructuralist criticism can show how power is exercised through discourse, including fictive discourse, how oppression works and where and how resistance might be possible. Poststructuralism, most particularly in its deconstructive forms, stresses the non-fixity and constant deferral of meaning. As a text-based theory, deconstruction is not interested in the implications of this for the reading subject beyond the primary assumption that this subject is not full, unitary or in control of meaning. However, as I have argued throughout this book, subjectivity is of key importance in the social processes and practices through which forms of class, race and gender power are exercised. We have to assume subjectivity in order to make sense of society and ourselves. The question is what modes of subjectivity are open to us and what they imply in political terms. Modes of subjectivity, like theories of society or versions of history, are temporary fixings in the on-going process in which any absolute meaning or truth is constantly deferred. The important point is to recognize the political implications of particular ways of fixing identity and meaning. From this perspective it is clear that we are far from achieving a society in which gender, race or class are non-issues.

In each of these struggles we need to define our objectives, both where they overlap and where they are different. As individuals our social locations will have implications for where and how we might act as part of a broader challenge to existing power relations. If feminism, for example, is primarily a set of discourses and political practices addressed to women, this is not the case for sexual politics as a whole. Men have hardly begun to look at the social construction of masculinity and the ways in which patriarchal power is exercised through subject positions open only, or most often, to them. If language and meanings are not naturally gender specific, as they cannot be from a poststructuralist perspective, nevertheless the enquiring subject is always already constructed emotionally and psychically by gendered patriarchal discourses. Moreover, power is invested in and exercised through her who speaks. Given the long history of the patriarchal silencing of women, it is crucial that women speak out for ourselves and occupy resistant subject positions while men work to deconstruct masculinity and its part in the exercising of patriarchal power.

The decentring of liberal-humanism, with its claims to full subjectivity and knowing rationality, in which *man* is the author of *his* thoughts and speech, is perhaps even more important in the deconstruction of masculinity than it is for women, who have never been fully included by this discourse. In the area of cultural and literary criticism it is imperative that we break the complicity of hegemonic forms of reading with liberal-humanist versions of subjectivity, knowledge and culture. This means breaking with traditional liberal-humanist disciplinary boundaries and introducing a perspective which attends to history promotes change.

For women active in the literary and educational institutions the task of transformation may seem overwhelming. It is important that we continue to be involved in and maintain supportive strategic links with the wider feminist movement, claiming and using the institutional power available to us but always with a view to subverting it and making resistant discourses and subject positions much more widely available. Outside formal educational and literary criticism, reading and writing are an apparently 'natural' part of everyday life. Their very naturalness is a condition of their effectivity in transmitting and reinforcing meanings and values, whether from the press, television or fiction. Yet the role of fiction in the Women's Liberation Movement since the late 1960s testifies to the transformative power of texts which raise questions of oppression and direct the reader towards new, more radical subject positions. Criticism's main sphere of operation has always been education, yet education is not restricted to formal schooling and higher education. Women's studies is a rapidly expanding area of adult education, important, if fraught with contradictions, and informal feminist reading groups remain an important feminist resource. There is no reason why critical writing should not have a much wider audience, provided it addresses the interests of the present in an accessible form. However, to read critically, in whatever context, we require a framework. This is both necessary and inescapable.

The particular feminist poststructuralist framework outlined in this book addresses subjectivity, discourse and power in a attempt to show that we need not take established meanings, values and power relations for granted. It is possible to demonstrate where they come from, whose interests they support, how they maintain sovereignty and where they are susceptible to specific pressures for change. It is a framework that can be applied to all forms of social and political practice. It is my hope in attempting to make this framework accessible that others will take it up and use it in the fight for change.

Notes

Chapter 1 Feminism and Theory

1 For an introduction to the issues with which the Women's Liberation Movement is concerned see *No Turning Back* (Feminist Anthology Collective, 1981), *Sweeping Statements* (Kanter et al. (eds), 1984) and the monthly magazine *Spare Rib*.

2 For a comprehensive account of types of feminist theory and politics up to but not including poststructuralist approaches see Jaggar, 1983. Liberal and socialist feminisms are relatively well represented among British publications. In the case of radical feminism, however, most of the influential texts are American and it is American authors that I discuss in this book. Yet even though radical feminism has not been taken up directly by many British writers it has had an important influence both on feminist politics and the development of socialist-feminist theories.

3 This is a key theme in the work of Mary Daly, Susan Griffin and Adrienne Rich. The need for new forms of feminist scholarship directed at women is argued in the recent feminist critique of the social sciences, *Breaking Out* (Stanley and Wise, 1983). However, this text does not move beyond untheorized women's experience.

4 Forms of psychoanalytic feminism, including French theory, are discussed in detail in chapter 3. A clear exposition of these writers can be found in the second half of *Sexual/Textual Politics* (Moi, 1985).

Chapter 2 Principles of Poststructuralism

1 For more on this see 'Wisewoman and Medicine Man: Changes in the Management of Childbirth' in Mitchell and Oakley (eds), 1976, pp. 17–58, and *Witches, Midwives and Nurses: a History of Women Healers*, Ehrenreich and English, 1973.

2 For a comprehensive discussion of liberal feminism see Jaggar, 1983. Janet Radcliffe Richards' *The Sceptical Feminist* (1982) is a clear example of liberal-feminist analysis.

3 *The Anti-social Family* (Barrett and MacIntosh, 1982) is an accessible example of socialist-feminist argument.

4 Examples of different types of theory used by socialist feminists can be found in Women's Studies Group, Centre for Contemporary Cultural Studies, 1978; Barrett, 1980; Brunt and Rowan, 1982; and Coward 1984.

5 See, for example Gayatri Spivak's essay 'Three Women's Texts' in *Critical Enquiry*, 12 (1), pp. 243–61.

6 For a comprehensive and clear introduction to deconstruction see *On Deconstruction* (Culler, 1983).

7 Althusser was writing here of ideology rather than discourse, but for poststructuralist theory the two terms become merged since, unlike much Marxist theory, poststructuralism has no concept of science as 'true' knowledge separate from ideology. It speaks rather of different forms of discourse with their own regularities, institutional locations, conditions of production and degrees of power within the social formation of which science is only one.

8 See, for example, *The German Ideology* (Marx, 1970), *The Manifesto of the Communist Party* (Marx, 1977) and *Capital, Volume One* (Marx, 1976).

9 For radical-feminist critiques of scientific writing see, for example, *Gyn/Ecology* (Daly, 1979) and *Woman and Nature* (Griffin, 1984).

Chapter 3 Feminist Poststructuralism and Psychoanalysis

1 The use of psychoanalysis in cultural analysis is discussed in the introductory text *Psychoanalytic Criticism: Theory in Practice* (Wright, 1984). Examples of feminist use of psychoanalysis can be found in *Female Desire* (Coward, 1984) and *Women and Film* (Kaplan, 1983) both of which are discussed in chapter 6.

See, in particular, the work of Juliet Mitchell and Jacqueline Rose listed in the bibliography.
3 For a treatment of the relationship between deconstruction and psychoanalysis see Culler, 1983, pp. 159–75.
4 For a brief overview of developments in psychoanalysis since Freud see the introductory essays in Mitchell and Rose, 1982.
5 See, for example the essay, 'Signifying Practice and Mode of Production', in the *Edinburgh 76 Magazine*, No. 1, 1976.

Chapter 4   Language and Subjectivity

1 This aspect of Marxist discourse is most clearly articulated in *The Origin of the Family, Private Property and the State* (Engels, 1972).
2 See, for example, *Femininity as Alienation* (Foreman, 1977). Non-humanist Marxism, however, rejects the idea of producing a general theory of human nature abstracted from the process of history. It argues that women and men are socially and historically produced as effects of social institutions and processes and the class struggle which underpins them. They have no essential nature from which they are alienated.
3 See, for example, *Sweeping Statements* (Kanter et al., 1984) or any issue of *Spare Rib*.
4 For an accessible overview of biological theories of gender difference see *Biological Politics* (Sayers, 1982).
5 *Feminism and Linguistic Theory* (Cameron, 1985) offers a clear and comprehensive account of non poststructuralist approaches to language and gender.
6 See, for example, the work of Adrienne Rich, Mary Daly and Susan Griffin.
7 This film was made in the USA in 1980 by Connie Field. It is distributed in Britain by The Other Cinema.

Chapter 5   Discourse, Power and Resistance

1 See Michel Foucault's *The Birth of the Clinic* (1973); *Discipline and Punish* (1979a); *The History of Sexuality, Volume One* (1981); and *The History of Sexuality, Volume Two* (1986).
2 It cannot be assumed, for example, that accounts of sexual difference which locate it in female and male biology are always used for

conservative ends. (For examples of feminist use of biological theory see Sayers, 1982.) However, it still remains the case that the implications of biological theory are ultimately conservative in so far as they fix women's nature.

Chapter 6   Feminist Critical Practice

1 See Lukács, 1963 and 1972; and Goldmann, 1964 and 1975.
2 For more on the incorporation of working-class writing see *Aspects of the Politics of Literature and Working-class Writing in Interwar Britain*, my unpublished Ph.D. thesis, University of Birmingham, 1984.
3 See the relevant essays in Jacobus, 1979; Showalter, 1985; Greene and Kahn, 1985; and Eagleton, 1986.
4 Examples of this kind of feminist criticism include Ellmann, 1979; Showalter, 1977; and Gilbert and Gubar, 1979.
5 See note 8.
6 See the discussion of Virginia Woolf in the introduction to *Sexual/ Textual Politics* (Moi, 1985).
7 See note 4 to ch. 3.
8 This is the dominant mode of feminist criticism found in the work of Elaine Showalter and Sandra Gilbert and Susan Gubar as well as the recent collections of feminist critical essays (Jacobus, 1979; Showalter, 1985; Greene and Kahn, 1985; and Eagleton, 1986).
9 For critiques of author-based criticism see Roland Barthes' 'The Death of the Author' (1977) and Michel Foucault's 'What is an Author?' (1979b).
10 For a brief, clear exposition of traditional as well as poststructuralist criticism see Catherine Belsey (1980).
11 GCSE and A-level examinations are set by the university examining boards for students aged 16 and 18 respectively. A-levels are required for entrance into higher education.
12 See *A Theory of Literary Production*, Pierre Macherey (1978).

Bibliography

Allen, Walter 1954: *The English Novel*. London: Phoenix House.

Althusser, Louis 1969: *For Marx*. Harmondsworth: Penguin.

1971: *Lenin and Philosophy and Other Essays*. London: New Left Books.

Baker Miller, Jean 1973: *Psychoanalysis and Women*. Harmondsworth: Penguin.

Barrett, Michèle 1980: *Women's Oppression Today*. London: Verso.

and McIntosh, Mary 1982: *The Anti-social Family*. London: Verso.

Barthes, Roland 1977: The Death of the Author. In *Image Music Text*, selected and translated by Stephen Heath. London: Fontana.

Belsey, Catherine 1980: *Critical Practice*. London: Methuen.

1985: *The Subject of Tragedy*. London: Methuen.

Benveniste, Emile 1971: *Problems in General Linguistics*. Miami: University of Miami Press.

Brunt, Rosalind and Rowan, Caroline (eds) 1982: *Feminism, Culture and Politics*. London: Lawrence and Wishart.

Cameron, Deborah 1985: *Feminism and Linguistic Theory*. London: Macmillan.

Chodorow, Nancy 1978: *The Reproduction of Mothering*. Berkeley: University of California Press.

Cixous, Hélène 1975: Sorties. From *La Jeune Née*. In Marks and de Courtivron, 1981, pp. 90–8.

1976: The Laugh of Medusa. From *Signs*, summer 1976. In Marks and de Courtivron, 1981, pp. 245–64.

Coward, Rosalind 1984: *Female Desire*. London: Paladin.

Culler, Jonathan 1983: *On Deconstruction*. London: Routledge and Kegan Paul.

Daly, Mary 1979: *Gyn/Ecology*. London: The Women's Press.

1984: *Pure Lust: Elemental Feminist Philosophy*. London: The Women's Press.

1985: *Beyond God the Father: Towards a Philosophy of Women's Liberation*. London: The Women's Press.

Dawkins, Richard 1976: *The Selfish Gene*. Oxford: Oxford University Press.

Derrida, Jacques 1973: *Speech and Phenomenon*. Evanston: North-western University Press.

1976: *Of Grammatology*. Baltimore: The John Hopkins University Press.

Eagleton, Mary (ed.) 1986: *Feminist Literary Theory*. Oxford: Blackwell.

Edinburgh 76 Magazine 1976, No. 1, Psycho-analysis, Cinema, Avant Garde. Edited by Phil Hardy, Claire Johnson and Paul Willeman. No imprint.

Ehrenreich, Barbara and English, Deirdre 1973: *Witches, Midwives and Nurses: a History of Women Healers*. Old Westbury: The Feminist Press.

Ellmann, Mary 1979: *Thinking About Women*. London: Virago.

Engels, Frederick 1972: *The Origin of the Family, Private Property and the State*. London: Lawrence and Wishart.

Fadermann, Lillian 1981: *Surpassing the Love of Men: Love Between Women from the Renaissance to the Present*. New York: Morrow.

Fairbairns, Zoë 1979: *Benefits*. London: Virago.

Felman, Shoshana 1975: Women and Madness: the Critical Phallacy. In *Diacritics*, 5 (4), pp. 2–10.

Feminist Anthology Collective 1981: *No Turning Back*. London: The Women's Press.

Firestone, Shulamith 1972: *The Dialectic of Sex*. London: Paladin.

Foreman, Ann 1977: *Femininity as Alienation: Women and the Family in Marxism and Psychoanalysis*. London: Pluto.

Foucault, Michel 1973: *The Birth of the Clinic*. London: Tavistock.

1978: *I, Pierre Rivière*. Harmondsworth: Peregrine.

1979a: *Discipline and Punish*. Harmondsworth: Penguin.

1979b: What is an Author? *Screen*, 20 (1), pp. 13–33.

1981: *The History of Sexuality, Volume One, An Introduction*. Harmondsworth: Pelican.

1986: *The History of Sexuality, Volume Two, The Use of Pleasure*. Harmondsworth: Viking.

Freud, Sigmund 1975: *The Psychopathology of Everyday Life*. Harmondsworth: Pelican.

1976: *The Interpretation of Dreams*. Harmondsworth: Pelican.

1977: *On Sexuality*. Harmondsworth: Penguin.

Gilbert, Sandra M. and Gubar, Susan 1979: *The Mad Woman in the Attic: the Woman Writer and the Nineteenth-Century Literary Imagination*. New Haven: Yale University Press.

Goldmann, Lucien 1964: *The Hidden God*. London: Routledge and Kegan Paul.

1975: *Towards a Sociology of the Novel*. London: Tavistock.

Griffin, Susan 1981: *Pornography and Silence: Culture's Revenge Against Nature*. London: The Women's Press.

1982: *Made From this Earth*. London: The Women's Press.

1984: *Woman and Nature: the Roaring Inside Her*. London: The Women's Press.

Greene, Gayle and Kahn, Coppelia 1985: *Making A Difference*. London: Methuen.

Greenwood, Walter 1933: *Love on the Dole*. London: Jonathan Cape.

Irigaray, Luce 1977: Women's Exile. *Ideology and Consciousness*, 1.

1985: *This sex which is not one*. New York: Cornell University Press.

Jacobus, Mary (ed.) 1979: *Women Writing and Writing About Women*. London: Croom Helm.

Jaggar, Alison 1983: *Feminist Politics and Human Nature*. Brighton: Harvester.

Kanter, Hannah; Lefanu, Sarah, Shah, Shaila and Spedding, Carole 1984: *Sweeping Statements*. London: The Women's Press.

Kaplan, E. Ann 1983: *Women and Film*. London: Methuen.

Kristeva, Julia 1974a: Oscillation between Power and Denial. From *Tel Quel*, Summer 1974. In Marks and de Courtivron, 1981, pp. 165–7.

1974b: Woman can never be defined. From *Tel Quel*, Autumn 1974. In Marks and de Courtivron, 1981, pp. 137–41.

1974c: Chinese Women Against the Tide. From *Tel Quel*, Autumn 1974. In Marks and de Courtivron, 1981, p. 240.

1977: About Chinese Women. From *Des Chinoises*, Urizen. In Marks and de Courtivron, 1981, p. 241.

1981: Women's Time. *Signs*, 7 (1), Chicago: University of Chicago Press.

1984: *Revolution in Poetic Language*. New York: Columbia University Press.

1986: *The Kristeva Reader* (edited by Toril Moi). Oxford: Blackwell.

Lacan, Jacques 1977: *Ecrits*. London: Tavistock.

Lukács, Georg 1963: *The Meaning of Contemporary Realism*. London: The Merlin Press.

1972: *Studies in European Realism.* London: The Merlin Press.
Macherey, Pierre 1978: *A Theory of Literary Production.* London: Routledge and Kegan Paul.
Marks, Elaine and de Courtivron, Isabelle 1981: *New French Feminisms.* Brighton: Harvester.
Marx, Karl 1970: *The German Ideology.* London: Lawrence and Wishart.
1976: *Capital, Volume One.* Harmondsworth: Penguin.
1977: *The Manifesto of the Communist Party.* Moscow: Progress.
Millett, Kate 1977: *Sexual Politics.* London: Virago.
Mitchell, Juliet 1975: *Psychoanalysis and Feminism.* Harmondsworth: Penguin.
1984: *Women: the Longest Revolution.* London: Virago.
and Oakley, Ann (eds) 1976: *The Rights and Wrongs of Women.* Harmondsworth: Penguin.
and Rose, Jacqueline 1982: *Feminine Sexuality, Jacques Lacan and the Ecole Freudienne.* London: Macmillan.
Moers, Ellen 1978, *Literary Women.* London, The Women's Press.
Moi, Toril 1985: *Sexual/Textual Politics.* London: Methuen.
Oakley, Ann 1972: *Sex, Gender and Society.* Aldershot: Temple Smith.
Piercy, Marge 1979: *Woman on the Edge of Time.* London: The Women's Press.
Radcliffe Richards, Janet 1982: *The Sceptical Feminist.* Harmondsworth: Penguin.
Rich, Adrienne 1977: *Of Woman Born: Motherhood as Experience and Institution.* London: Virago.
1981: *Compulsory Heterosexuality and Lesbian Experience.* London: Onlywomen Press.
1980: *On Lies, Secrets, Silence.* London: Virago.
Rosaldo, Michelle Zimbalist and Lamphere, Louise 1974: *Women, Culture and Society.* Stanford: Stanford University Press.
Sayers, Janet 1982: *Biological Politics.* London, Tavistock.
Saussure, Ferdinand de 1974: *A Course in General Linguisitics.* London: Fontana.
Showalter, Elaine 1977: *A Literature of Their Own: Women Novelists from Brontë to Lessing.* New Jersey: Princeton University Press.
(ed.) 1985: *The New Feminist Criticism.* London, Virago.
Spare Rib n.d.: women's liberation magazine, monthly. London.
Spivak, Gayatri 1985: 3 Women's Texts. *Critical Enquiry,* 12 (1), pp. 243–61. Chicago: University of Chicago Press.
Stanley, Liz and Wise, Sue 1983: *Breaking Out: Feminist Consciousness and Feminist Research.* London: Routledge and Kegan Paul.

Women's Studies Group, Centre for Contemporary Cultural Studies
　　1978: *Women Take Issue*. London: Hutchinson.
Wright, Elizabeth 1984: *Psychoanalytic Criticism: Theory in Practice*.
　　London: Methuen.

Index